On the Controversies

which, in the previous time, have been raised and debated concerning certain Articles of the Augsburg Confession,

THE JUDGMENT

of

Dr. Martin Chemnitz,
Superintendent of the Church of Brunswick

published by

Polycarp Leyser,
Doctor of Theology and Pastor of the Church at Wittenberg

With privilege.

Wittenberg
Printed by Simon Gronenberg.
1594

Repristination Press
Malone, Texas

Original title: *De Controversiis Quibusdam, quae superiori tempore, circa quosdam Augustanae Confessionis Articulos...* (1594). Translation © 2024 by Repristination Press. All rights reserved by Repristination Press. No part of this publication may be reproduced, stored in a retrieval system, or transmitted in any form or by any means, electronic, mechanical, photocopying or otherwise without the prior written permission of Repristination Press.

First edition, October 2024.

REPRISTINATION PRESS
716 HCR 3424 E
MALONE, TEXAS 76660

www.repristinationpress.com

ISBN (10) 1-891469-85-1
ISBN (13) 978-1-891469-85-5

Table of Contents

Foreword to the English Translation	5
Foreword by Polycarp Leyser	7
I. On a Definite Body of Doctrine.	15
II. On the Word. [περὶ τοῦ λόγου.]	19
III. On the Free Will.	27
IV. On External Discipline or the Righteousness of the Flesh.	35
V. On the Capacity of the Unregenerate Free Will to Initiate and Accomplish Spiritual Motions in Conversion or Renewal.	49
VI. On the Definition of the Gospel.	57
VII. On the Common Definition, That the Gospel is the Preaching of Repentance and the Forgiveness of Sins.	65
VIII. On the Article of Justification	75
IX. On Good Works.	91
X. On Adiaphora.	111

4

Foreword.

We have undertaken the translation and publication of this volume because it is our belief that it is of use to the Church for attaining a more complete understanding the confession of the Formula of Concord published in the *Book of Concord* (1580). Like Jacob Andreae's *Six Christian Sermons on the Divisions Which Have Continued to Surface Among the Theologians of the Augsburg Confession from 1548 until This Year 1573**, Martin Chemnitz's *On the Controversies* anticipates the argumentation set forth in various articles of the Formula of Concord.

In general, footnotes have been kept to a minimum, although a few have been added for the sake of clarity, and to guide the reader to the pertinent portion of the Formula of Concord where the various controversies are definitively addressed.

We note that certain portions of this work were translated for *Sources and Contexts of The Book of Concord*.** However, because that volume excluded so much of Chemnitz's work,*** it was decided that it was necessary to publish the entire volume to allow readers access to the full shape of Chemnitz's overall argument. Furthermore, we have chosen not to consult the translation in *Sources and Contexts* so as to allow for a fresh approach to the text. This choice is not intended as any sort of disparagement of the previous excerpted translation which was executed by scholars who are

* Published in English translation as *Andreae and the Formula of Concord: Six Sermons on the Way to Lutheran Unity*, trans. by Robert Kolb (St. Louis: Concordia Publishing House, 1977).
** ed. by Robert Kolb and James A. Nestingen, (Minneapolis: Fortress Press, 2001). The work in question was translated by J.A.O. Preus and Robert Kolb.
*** Chapters II, IV, V, VI, VII, IX and X are entirely omitted; ellipses in the text indication omissions in the published chapters.

worthy of the utmost respect. Rather, since we have approached the work with the intention of translating it in its entirety, it was deemed prudent to undertake the task without the biases which reference to the previous translation would inherently impart.

We are grateful to the efforts of Anastasia Heiser, M.A., who rendered invaluable assistance as a Latinist and editorial assistant in correcting some of the multitude of shortcomings in the manuscript. However, as in all such undertakings, the translator alone is responsible for shortcomings in the difficult task of allowing Chemnitz to speak to an anglophone age.

Rt. Rev. James D. Heiser
Bishop, the ELDoNA
19th Sunday after Trinity, A.D. 2024

To the man of Ancient and Primary Nobility, distinguished in piety, virtue and wisdom, Lord Georgius de Sleinitz, hereditary Lord in Stauchitz, Electoral Saxon Counselor, his most honorable Lord,

Polycarpus Leyser, D.
Wishes health in the Lord.

Just as in human affairs, nothing is sweeter or more delightful, and nothing more worthy of pursuit than the heavenly doctrine, by which God, emerging from His secret abode, has revealed Himself and His will with immense mercy to the human race, for the sake of their eternal salvation, so nothing is sadder, nothing more lamentable to good minds and moderate spirits, than to see the form of this heavenly doctrine, once rightly established, torn apart in the Church by either manifest corruptions or unnecessary disputes, and everything thrown into turmoil and confusion by contentions. For in those most sorrowful confusions of opinions and disputes, not only are many good minds turned away from the study of heavenly doctrine, but men and princely figures are so disturbed and offended that they become more estranged in spirit towards religion.

And this is the old trick of the devil, the immortal enemy of mortals, which he first accomplishes through contentious men by disturbing the purity and consensus of doctrine in the Church, and then he arouses Sophists who, under the pretext of εἰρκνοφιλία (a love of peace), tend to confuse and reconcile all opinions into one, or, from an innate arrogance, are accustomed to mock all religions, so that in this way Epicureanism and atheism, in which vices the devil takes the greatest delight, may be spread throughout the world.

8

Thus, formerly, Libanius*, a famous Sophist at the time, by highlighting and exaggerating the sad spectacle of divisions in the Church, so alienated the mind of Emperor Julian from the Christian religion that he returned to paganism with a clear apostasy because he was persuaded, due to the battles and contentions within the Church, that the entire doctrine of the Church had no certainty. And Ammianus** reports about Julian that he once convened the bishops of various sects, along with the people divided into various opinions, all together within the palace, and addressed them in this manner: That with civil discord thus quelled, in the matter of religion, each person, without hindrance, might fearlessly serve his own queen, indicating that he granted the freedom to freely and without punishment conceive and defend whatever opinion one might wish concerning religion.

This happened in the time of Julian. But how many today among Christians do we think there are, who, besides being men of various learning, wisdom, eloquence, extensive experience in [political] affairs, and other distinguished gifts, are outstanding; yet, with regard to religion, either they mock all religions altogether, or they think it matters not what belief one follows in the matter of religion? Hence, to the leading men, some suggest, others demand, that dissenters be suppressed by royal hand; others, that no theologian be listened to anymore; others, that by some Syncretism all controversies be removed; others, that the refutation and censure of various opinions be forbidden; others, that the more sincere be expelled and the more turbulent be kept, if by these means the foundations of the Church might be undermined, or even overturned;

---

* Libanus (A.D. 314–394) was a Sophist rhetorician from Antioch who taught at Constantinople for a number of years, befriending Julian. He composed a series of orations which alienated Julian from the Christian faith.

** Ammianus Marcellinus (A.D. 330–ca. 391) wrote *Res gestae*, a history of Rome from A.D. 96 to the Battle of Adrianople in 378. Only the portion of his history covering the period from 353 to 378 survives.

others, (which is horrendous to say and hear) that all mention of Christ and the Gospel be forbidden to the ministers of the Word. Indeed, these are the mockeries of Satan, by which they ridicule Christ's suffering and agonizing on the cross, and to the same in the utmost tortures, and in the greatest pains, they offer vinegar mixed with gall.

But this malice of Satan must be countered in the way that the Lord has prescribed in His Word. For from His divine Word—not from the thoughts of reason, nor from the opinions of the sons of this age—must judgment be formed against such tumults.

And indeed, Scripture encourages both teachers and students to strive for true, pious, and healthful concord, that they may be of the same mind, hold the same judgment, feel the same, and speak the same. {1 Cor. 3}* And to this exhortation everyone ought rightly to give place, especially since Paul says that whoever disturbs the Church will carry his own judgment, whoever he may be. {Gal. 5} And Christ the Savior pronounces a dreadful woe to those who cause scandal, even to the least among the believers. {Mat. 18}

But because of Satan's malice, we can never hope for such concord or peace in which no contention would interpose itself in the Church. For the same Holy Scripture predicts that it will come to pass that at all times, and in various ways, the heavenly doctrine will be attacked in this world and opposed by presumptuous minds. Indeed, where there is the Lord's field, there the enemy sows tares {Matthew 13}; where there are sheep, there wolves roam {John 10}; where your treasure is kept, there thieves dig to steal it {Matthew 6}. Therefore, we must not pretend as if the purity of doctrine can be retained in the Church without conflicts. Rather, everyone should learn from Scripture how they ought to conduct themselves piously when conflicts and contentions arise.

---
* Please note: text enclosed in this fashion ({}) indicates marginal notations.

Therefore, when new tumults arise, Paul instructs teachers to cling so firmly to sound doctrine that they not only faithfully present it pure and uncorrupted to others, but also severely rebuke those who contradict {Titus 1}, and if anyone dares to change or corrupt the form of sound words, they should courageously refute them. {1 Timothy 3} The Savior also declares that those are not faithful shepherds, but treacherous hirelings, who indeed teach correctly, but do not stand against the wolf coming with false doctrine, nor do they warn the little sheep to be wary. {John 10} Therefore, those clever individuals who, upon the arising of ecclesiastical conflict, advise silencing both parties—both the one defending pure doctrine and the other introducing novelties [καινοφανίας] and empty talk [κενοφωνίας]—should not be heeded, and if the teachers of truth do not comply, they immediately accuse them of having transgressed the decrees of the magistrate. But the clamor of these individuals should not be regarded; rather, on the contrary, the words of Peter should be thundered and proclaimed in their ears: "We must obey God rather than men." {Acts 8}

But to the learners, Paul says, "I urge you, watch those who cause divisions and offenses contrary to the doctrine you have learned and turn away from them." {Rom. 16} And again: "Pray for us, that we may be delivered from unreasonable and wicked men: for not all have faith." {2 The. 3} Therefore, listeners should separate themselves from those who, out of pride and a love of contention, seek to innovate anything against the usual, accepted, and Scripturally-confirmed doctrine. For those among the listeners who are ambidextrous, fostering the interests of both parties, often become odious to both God and men. Certainly, the Son of God Himself, when He saw some wanting to be idle spectators, or (as they are called) 'Neutrals' in the conflicts that arose between Him and the Pharisees, clearly pronounced, "He who is not with Me is against Me," and, "He who does not gather with Me, scatters." {Luke 11}

Furthermore, what roles political magistrates should play in such tumults are beautifully demonstrated by the examples of Jehoshaphat, Hezekiah, and Josiah, who, not with private and contentious, but with public authority, and not to show off their power, but to strengthen faith, either restored the collapsed state of religion or corrected the depraved and corrupted one by removing the disruptors. These examples were followed by Christian Emperors Constantine the Great[*], Theodosius II[**], Marcian[***], and others, who allowed themselves to be no less concerned with promoting the purity of doctrine in the Church than with administering peace and justice in the Empire. And because this care of the magistrate is bounded by certain limits, God has always been accustomed to add to pious rulers faithful and sincerity-loving ministers, whether ecclesiastical or political, who would advise and suggest how everything should be done according to the prescribed standard and rule of divine Law. Thus we read that Gad and Nathan were with David, Azariah son of Obed with Asa, Isaiah with Hezekiah, Hilkiah with Josiah, and others, who, with joint effort and unanimous endeavor, focused on ensuring that the state of the Church retained its luster according to the prescription of the divine Word, and the license to contend and contradict was justly restrained.

Into this remembrance, Most Noble Lord, I have entered, while at the same time considering the publication of a mediating treatise, in which the most distinguished theologian of our times,

---

[*] Constantine the Great (A.D. 272–337) was emperor from A.D. 307, issued the Edict of Milan in 313, legalizing the Church. He convened the Council of Nicea in 325 to address the division in the Church occasioned by the Arian heresy.
[**] Theodosius (A.D. 401–450), convened the Council of Ephesus in 431.
[***] Marcian (A.D. 392–457), convened the Council of Chalecedon in 451. All three emperors are presented by Leyser as supreme magistrates who provided the Church with opportunities for a clear confession of the teachings of Holy Scripture in Ecumenical Councils.

Dr. Martin Chemnitz, once the most vigilant Superintendent of the Church of Brunswick, laid out his judgment on the controversies of earlier times, and I contemplate the new struggle that is stirred up against us just as the healthier doctrine is restored and the Church is at peace. For I do not think that anyone can fault me if I publicly declare that I grieve over this situation, likened to the sorrow of Joseph. I grieve deeply in the name of these regions and the entire Church because the simplicity of the received and sound form of doctrine is entangled and tainted; because the Holy Spirit is saddened in many hearts; because the invocation and the united effort to build up the Church are disturbed; because finally, seeds are scattered from which greater evils may arise, unless these wounds are legitimately and quickly healed and cured. Would that God soon, with all the heat of contentions calmed, restore to our schools and churches a pious, serene, tranquil, and healthful concord.

Meanwhile, whenever some, due to the emergence of new ecclesiastical conflicts, either because of their role or the impulse of conscience, cannot remain silent but are compelled to express their opinion and contradict the Innovators, they have an excellent example to follow, expressed by Dr. Chemnitz in this treatise. He does not burden those who disagree with carts of insults, nor does he lead them into hatred of others with fabricated slanders, nor does he cunningly entangle them in ruin; but setting aside persons, he tends to examine their opinion according to the Word of God and, without any bitterness, regularly pronounces what is in harmony and conformity with the divine oracles. If this example were followed by more, while it is doubtful that the very first inventors of new opinions could be brought back to the right path, there is no doubt that many good people, ensnared by their traps, could be freed and won back.

I wished, however, to publish this treatise at this very time, when I am following and entering into the most illustrious Elector's court from the renowned Republic of Brunswick and the highly praised University of Wittenberg, for various reasons, but also for this one: To publicly testify before the Church of Christ that I am not bringing any new type of doctrine, even regarding the controversial articles of our religion—nor any kind of Swabian Theology* (as I hear some jest, either seriously or facetiously)—but firmly standing on that doctrine which true Saxony has at all times most steadfastly defended, and which Meissen, whenever it was knowingly Lutheran and purified from Calvinist dregs, has gratefully embraced and revered. If I were to bring a different doctrine, by Apostolic decree I myself would affirm that not even a greeting should be offered to me. {2 John} For not even an angel from heaven should be listened to if he preaches a gospel other than what we have received. {Gal. 1} But if I steadfastly press on in presenting sound doctrine in the footsteps of those who have always been regarded and found to be orthodox in these churches, what harm is it to me that I have come from another region? For in Christ Jesus, there is neither Gentile nor Jew, neither male nor female, neither Barbarian nor Scythian, neither Saxon nor Swabian, neither slave nor free, But Christ is all, and in all. {Col. 3}

To your most esteemed name, Most Noble Lord GEORGE OF SLEINITZ, I wished to dedicate this treatise, the result of another's labor, because I have come to know from trustworthy witnesses, and have indeed experienced myself, that you meticulously examine theological controversies, steadfastly and precisely adhere to the orthodox opinion, and embrace and support all sincere theo-

---

* Friedrich Wilhelm I (1562–1602) brought Aegidius Hunnius (1550–1603) to Wittenberg in 1592, and Hunnius and Leyser were close friends and allies. Hunnius was closely identified with Johann Brenz's Swabian Theology. Furthermore, such attacks on Leyser are aimed at his having been born in southern Germany; Saxons of dubious confession played the ethnic 'card' against him.

logians with a sincere affection of the heart. Therefore, in order to enhance and affirm this zeal for piety and affection of charity in Your Nobility from my own position, I deemed this dedication to be a fitting means.

The most noble Sleinitz family has always had (as have other illustrious families of these regions, concerning whom I would not wish to detract anything in this regard) distinguished supporters and patrons of purer doctrine, among whom, Lord THEODORIC, Lord of Hoff and Bornitz, and Lord WOLFGANG ALBERT, your own brother, hold not the least significant roles, as is most certain by the testimony of all good people. Therefore, to retain many such individuals and for posterity to also have them, God must be prayed to, and you Sleinitzes will allow nothing to be desired in yourselves. We who handle sacred matters will strive to deserve all piety, observance, and services towards you and those like you, and will further endeavor to bind ourselves to you.

I pray with all my heart to God the Father that, for the sake of His only begotten Son, by the Holy Spirit, He may guide and generously bless your Most Illustrious house throughout life, so that without interruption, it may live and act εὐσεβῶς (piously) towards God, δικαίως (righteously) towards neighbor, and σωφρόνως (temperately) towards itself, for His glory, the honor of the most noble family, and the benefit of the entire country. Amen.

Written in Dresden, in the year 1594, on the 16th of July, on which day, in the year 1576, along with the most celebrated theologian, the most noble AEGIDIUS HUNNIUS, my brother in Christ to be honored, I was adorned with the doctoral title and honor by the teachers of Tübingen.

On Certain Controversies,
which in Earlier Times,
Regarding Some Articles of the Augsburg Confession,
Were Stirred and Debated,

JUDGMENT

of Dr. MARTIN CHEMNITZ,
Superintendent of the Church of Brunswick.

I.
On a Definite Body of Doctrine.

Some discuss these controversies in such a way that they think they have done well if they can reconcile conflicting opinions by any means of color and artifice. Others, on the contrary, by always stirring up new and often unnecessary disputes, seem to aim to gradually surrender the Body of Doctrine [*corpus doctrinae*], established in a moderately suitable form, to our destruction. They have testified that they embrace the Augsburg Confession, presented to the Emperor, and the Apology that was added to it. Then, in the year 1537, the Smalcald Articles were written by LUTHER*, in the name of our churches, and the reasons why those Articles were written and received by our people after the Confession are recounted by LUTHER himself in the preface; namely, because both at Augsburg and afterwards, conciliations were often attempted, with many believing that some things in the articles of the Augsburg Confession could be relaxed and conced-

---

* Leyser (presumably following Chemnitz) often prints Martin Luther's name in all caps, presumably to emphasize the significance of the Reformer's thought to the entire discussion. We have retained this stylistic touch to retain the sense of emphasis intended by the author.

ed to the Papists. Moreover, because fanatics and sectarians under the pretext of LUTHER were selling their delusions to the less educated, as if LUTHER understood the doctrine of the Augsburg Confession differently; therefore, the Smalcald Articles were written to serve both as a confirmation and as a true, certain, and perpetual declaration of the Augsburg Confession: How its sentiment was conveyed and understood in all our churches during LUTHER's lifetime. And it is understood from the subscriptions, that whereas previously only a few had subscribed to the confession, it is here understood that the Augsburg Confession, its Apology, and the attached declaration in the Smalcald Articles were approved and received as the symbol and correct form of doctrine by all our churches, so that in this way it would stand in opposition to both the papal council and all fanatics.

Just as the ancients had their symbols, in which, against the corruptions of heretics, the form and ὑποτύπωσις (pattern) of sound words were set forth for teachers and learners, so the body of doctrine of our churches, which we judge to be the true and perpetual sentiment of the Prophetic and Apostolic writings, in that sense which is expressed in the approved symbols, is this: The Augsburg Confession, its Apology, and the Smalcald Articles. And there are true and serious reasons why we wish the Smalcald Articles to be added, for some things are explained more fully there, such as concerning the Pope, the power of Bishops, Zwinglianism, Transubstantiation, and sins that drive out the Holy Spirit.[*]

Moreover, it has often been called into dispute and conflict by our papal adversaries that the copies of the Augsburg Confession do not agree with each other but vary considerably, as the comparison of the editions from the years 1530, 1531, 1537, and

---

[*] Chemnitz, and his Superintendent, Joachim Mörlin, were among those contending at the Diet of Naumberg (1561) for the Smalcald Articles to be formally included as a Lutheran symbol. The current work was published in the aftermath of the diet.

1542 testifies. The same question is also debated among our own [theologians] with great contention. And it is a matter of great importance, so that it is necessary to establish something correct about this, both because of the present conflicts and especially for the sake of posterity. Otherwise, new disputes will always be initiated under the pretext of another edition [of the Augsburg Confession].

Calvin and his followers eagerly seize the tenth article in the edition of the Year 1542 (because he sees it as a shoe which he could also easily fit to Zwingli's foot). However, he disapproves and rejects the article as it was presented to the Emperor, and as it appears in the edition of the Year 1531, because it affirms that the body of Christ is truly present in the Supper, and disapproves of those who teach otherwise.

Therefore, careful provision must be made to avoid dangerously disturbing the churches without serious cause. The edition of the Year 1531 cannot and should not be rejected, for this is the true Augsburg Confession, as it was presented to Emperor Charles in the Year 1530, and it is always cited in this manner. Also, all of our churches subscribed to this edition at Smalcald in 1537. Nor do I see how the edition of 1542 can be usefully and rightly rejected and condemned. For when the Colloquy of Hagenau was arranged for 1542, and it was judged to be useful to present the body and form of doctrine of our churches as the subject matter of the colloquy, it was published that year in Wittenberg, with a fuller declaration added in some places. That edition was also presented in Worms in the same year, under the name of the Augsburg Confession. The same edition was opposed to the adversaries at the Colloquy of Regensburg as the form of doctrine of our churches. And this was done with the advice, approval, and consent of LUTHER. Thus, in the Year 1546 and thereafter in all assemblies and actions concerning religion, our side referred to this edition, which they called the Augsburg Confession. Nor can it be demonstrated that there is anything in the way of errors or corruptions in those declarations that were added in the edition of 1542, except for the mutilation in the tenth article. Indeed, by Cochlaeus at Worms in 1540 and Pighius in 1541 at Regensburg, it was taken seriously that many articles had gained somewhat more light with the fuller declaration. From this, they saw true sentiments being more illuminated, and the shame of the Babylonian Thais being more clearly exposed, and they would have preferred to simply retain the edition of 1531, as their writings testify. However, since the edition of 1540 is widely circulated and the first edition of 1531 is unknown to most [people] and scarcely ever seen, and it [i.e., the edition of 1540] contains nothing false but only some necessary clarifications, I do not see how it can be entirely or simply rejected and condemned without disturbing the churches. Therefore, it seems most advisable that the edition of 1531 be restored to the churches and commended as being of full and primary authority. The edition of 1540 should also be retained as a declaration, which should not conflict, but be in all respects consistent with the first edition. The tenth article should be restored so that the mention of the elements remains and the rest from the first edition is added. Also, Paul's passage in the tenth article of the Apology should be restored, although what is added there from the Greek canon and from the Vulgate about the change could be softened. Yet since the Vulgate asserts Transubstantiation clearly and grossly, it would be better to omit those passages, or to correctly declare them in such a way that Transubstantiation is clearly rejected. In this manner, the Body of Doctrine would remain correct, provision would be made for posterity, and the churches would not be disturbed.*

---

* Chemnitz's moderate position regarding receptions of various editions of the Augsburg Confession would be superseded by the clear subscription to "our symbol for this time, the first, unaltered Augsburg Confession, which was delivered to Emperor Charles V at Augsburg in 1530 during the great diet of the empire" (FC Epitome ¶4).

II.
On the Word. [περὶ τοῦ λόγου.]*

It is certain in the true Church that τοῦ λόγου (the Word) in John does not signify the external ministry, nor is the very Person of the Father, in respect to revelation, called λόγον (the Word); but it is to be understood as the second Person of the Trinity, distinct from the Father and the Holy Spirit. And it is an article of faith that this λόγος (Word) is the Son of God, ὁμοούσιος (of the same substance), who was from the Father before all ages, and it is necessary that this be expressly explained and set forth in the Church.

For Servetus** craftily played with the testimonies of Irenaeus from chapters 47 and 48 of book 2***. The words of Irenaeus are: "God is entirely mind, entirely λόγος (Word), entirely Spirit in action, entirely light. Likewise, His thought is λόγος, and λόγος is mind, and encompassing all, this very mind is the Father." From this, Servetus constructs the argument that antiquity did not perceive the λόγος to be a self-subsisting Person distinct from the Father, but that the λόγος is called one and the same Person as the Father in this respect: that He reveals His thoughts by speaking,

---

* The initial focus of this chapter primarily on Arian and Antitrinitarian theologians. Such heretics are denounced in the concluding paragraphs of Article XII of the Formula of Concord, both in the Epitome (XII:28–29) and Solid Declaration (XII:36–39). However, the Christological content of this chapter is also related to Article VIII of the Formula of Concord.
** Michael Servetus (1511–1553) was an Antitrinitarian theologian who was burned at the stake by Calvinists. Servetus is not specifically named in the Formula of Concord.
*** St. Irenaeus of Lyons (A.D. 130–202) served as an early bishop of Lyons, but is remembered today primarily as the author of *Adversus Haereses*, a five volume work dedicated primarily to refuting the Christological errors of the Gnostics.

and the same Person of the Father is named the Holy Spirit in respect to operation, and thus there is only one Person in the divinity, which, however, in different respects, has different names. Therefore, since the same testimonies of Irenaeus are now opposed in this debate, to avoid any occasion for error, a declaration must be sought and given to maintain the article: That the λόγος is a divine Person, ὁμοούσιος (of the same substance), self-subsisting and distinct from the Father and the Holy Spirit.

Regarding the question of the manner of generation, the response of Nazianzen[*] is true: "The generation of God is to be honored in silence, and indeed, that the Son was begotten is a great thing for you to have learned; but how He was begotten is not even known to the angels themselves, let alone granted to you. Furthermore, if you cannot depart without an answer to your question ("how"), I respond that He was begotten in the manner known to the Father who begot and the Son who was begotten. What is more sublime than this is covered by a cloud, so that it may easily escape the blinding eyes of your intellect." The same [Nazianzen], when pressed with that question to specify the difference between *being begotten* and *proceeding*, replied, "Tell me what generation is, and I will tell you what procession is, so we both may go mad by prying into the secrets of God." As for how much Scripture has revealed to us about these great mysteries, it is to be thought upon reverently and with a grateful mind, although we cannot attain perfect knowledge of these mysteries in this life. "For we know in part, and we prophesy in part" (1 Cor. 13:9). Likewise, verse 12: "We see through a glass, darkly."

Therefore, the thoughts of the ancients on the appellations that are attributed to the Son of God according to divinity in

---

[*] Gregory of Nazianzus (A.D. 329–390), bishop of Nazianzus and one of the Capadocian Fathers, is revered as among the most important Trinitarian theologians of the early church. His writings were of great significance at the Council of Ephesus (A.D. 431) and the Council of Chalcedon (A.D. 4510).

Scripture are pious and learned. For the *knowledge* of God that we have in this life is called the *name* of God.

Therefore, the ancients deemed it worthwhile to devote some effort to considering those appellations. And because in Heb. 1:3, the Son is called the ἀπαύγασμα (radiance) of the δόξης (glory) of God, the Nicene Fathers proposed this certain image for contemplating the generation of the Son of God: "God from God, light from light." Indeed, they were not so foolish as to think that the mystery of divine generation could be perfectly shown by this image, as if the manner of the Son's generation was exactly like how we see light from light either ignited or shining forth. But because they saw that this image could somehow clarify the doctrine of the Trinity for the less learned, especially since they felt that such appellations, taken from the cause of things, were attributed to the Son of God in Scripture not without reason. Ambrose adapts the similarity thus: "Just as it cannot be comprehended that the radiance is later than the light or the light older than the radiance, nor can they be separated." So also Augustine speaks of the incarnation, saying that the light is known through the radiance, and the weak eyes of mortals can more easily bear the radiance than the source of light. Thus, the Father is known through the Son, etc. Justin[*] says, "The Son was begotten by the Father, just as light (φῶς) shone forth from light (φωτός)." And he adds, "For this image is suitable to present coeternity, the unity of essence, and that the Son was begotten without suffering, not through flow, cutting, or separation of substance."

If someone should want to harshly criticize these pious thoughts of the ancients, as there might not be a lack of opportunities for sharp criticism, that person would neither be acting piously nor rightly.

---

[*] Justin Martyr (A.D. 100–165) is remember primarily for three works, his *First* and *Second Apology*, and his *Dialogue with Trypho*.

In the same way, the Son is called λόγος in John 1. This Word signifies both the external and internal word, that is, thought. He is also called the Image in Col. 1:15 and the exact representation of the Father's substance in Heb. 1:3. Just as the ancients took the appellation of radiance from Heb. 1:3 and derived from it the image of light from light for a certain non-impious and not faulty declaration of the doctrine concerning the Son of God, so also, because Scripture describes the divinity of the Son of God with appellations taken from the nature of the human mind, merely for the sake of clarification, they proposed to themselves the image of the human mind, which tends to generate images through thinking, so that the Word might be the likeness and exact representation of the human mind, just as Augustine takes great delight in this thought, seeking and considering traces of the Trinity in the human mind. And indeed, in explaining this appellation, they particularly considered the office, that He is the Person who brings forth from the secret counsel of God the decree about the redemption of mankind, and that He is present in His ministry with His efficacy.

However, they note that the Son is called λόγος (Word), not only from the time when He began to issue promises and speak with the fathers, but He has been λόγος with God from eternity (John 1:2). And He is called λόγος not only in relation to us, but also in relation to the Father, of whom He is the λόγος. Therefore, for a certain non-impious declaration about the Trinity, they used this image of the human mind. And they employed both analogies of the word: the internal, that is, thought, and the external, i.e., speech, which in men is generated by thought and is the image of what is thought. They did not attribute more to this image than what comparisons from human to divine usually hold, namely, that the Son is called λόγος because He is the image of the Father, but not as our thought or our word is a fading image; rather, λόγος is the exact representation of the Father's substance; that is, the

Father shares His essence with His image. And these three appellations in John 1:1, Col. 1:15, and Hebrews 1:3, lead us straightforwardly to these thoughts.

Nor is Philip [Melanchthon]'s interpretation new, but the ancients spoke in this way. Nor did they draw these thoughts from physics, but from the appellations taken from the nature of the human mind, which Scripture attributes to the Son of God not without reason. Thus, Basil[*] on page 209 [in his sermon on the words: "In the beginning was the Word"] piously and learnedly expounds the appellation λόγος[**]: "Why the Word? To show what proceeds from the mind. Why, I say, the Word? Because it is the image of the Begetter, displaying in itself the entirety of the Begetter, not dividing any part from it, and being perfect in itself, just like our word, which reflects the image of our entire thought. For what we know according to the heart, we express in word. And what we speak has a model in what we think in the heart." And Nazianzen says[***]: "He is called the Word because His relation to the Father is like that of speech to the mind, not only because this generation is devoid of affections, but also because of their union and the role of interpretation." Athanasius also uses this analogy in his second sermon against the Arians, on folio 140, and often employs this argument to prove the eternity of the Father and the Son, because the Father is not a mind without reason (νοῦς ἄλογος), nor is the Son a word without mind (λόγος ἀνοῦς). He also cites a lengthy statement from Dionysius of Alexandria about this analogy of the human mind, on folio 305. I am inclined to include these words: "Our mind brings forth a word from itself, and each derives its own properties from the other and occu-

---

[*] St. Basil of Caesarea (A.D. 330–378), another of the Cappadocian fathers, a proponent of Nicene orthodoxy over against the Arian heresy.
[**] Chemnitz provides the quotation in Greek, and then offers his own translation into Latin. Our translation is from Chemnitz's Latin text.
[***] As with Basil, Chemnitz offers the quotation in Greek before offering his translation. Our translation is from Chemnitz's Latin.

pies a distinct place, while the one resides in the heart, the other on the tongue and in the mouth, and has its own movement, but not so that they are separated and lack each other, nor is the mind irrational, that is, without the word and without reason, nor is the word mindless, that is, without a mind, but the mind makes the word, and appears in the word, and the word declares the mind, which consists in it, and the mind is as if the word were at rest. The word, however, is as if the mind were springing forth, and the mind passes into the word, but the word insinuates the mind into the hearers. And thus the mind is placed in the minds of the hearers, entering together with the word, and the mind is, because it exists by itself as the father of the word. But the word is like the son of the mind: as it is impossible to have existed before the mind, so it is by no means without it, but existed together with it, and was brought forth from it. In the same way, the greatest Father, and entirely the mind, has His Son, the Word, as the interpreter and messenger of Himself." Justin also uses the same analogy in [his *Dialogue with*] *Trypho*, where he explains why the Son is named λόγος. So also Hilary* says, "The word of thought is eternal, for He who thinks is eternal." And Cyprian in the exposition of the Creed among other images and analogies of the Trinity also uses that of the human mind generating the word. In Augustine, indeed, there are very many such statements.

 LUTHER does not condemn these images or likenesses of the ancients, but in his commentary on the first chapter of Genesis, he says, "Good fathers such as Augustine and Hilary also took pleasure in such thoughts." And LUTHER demonstrates in his *Postil* how these images, although weak and imperfect for expressing the generation of the Son, nevertheless can be piously adapted to explain the doctrine of this mystery.

---

* Hilary of Portiers (A.D. 310–367), was bishop of Portiers and an important Western theologian who contended with the Arians. He was the author of *De Trinitate* and the most important Western theologian prior to St. Ambrose.

Therefore, since these [likenesses] are not new, nor do they pose any inconvenience when understood correctly, those who, without necessary reasons, not only vehemently criticize these kinds of images but also equate them with the scandalous and blasphemous opinions of Saturninus, Basilides*, and the like, are not acting rightly.

This would indeed be done rightly and beneficially if, for the sake of clarification, such necessary admonitions were candidly added in these discussions, namely, that these images are weak and imperfect likenesses, which should not be twisted to scrutinize the mystery of divine generation, beyond and outside the word, as Athanasius often warns and shows, pointing out the difference between the word of man and the λόγος of God. Yet, they are still employed to provide a somewhat cruder explanation of the pious doctrine concerning the Son of God revealed in the Scriptures. And they are used on the basis that Scripture employs such appellations, which are taken from images in the natural world. Nevertheless, that remains which the ancients apply to this question: "Who shall declare his generation?" Also, it is rightly done when minds are drawn away from the speculation of the arcane generation in the divine to a more useful contemplation of Christ's offices in the Church.

The admonition must also necessarily be added that there should be a measure in such questions, not to wander beyond the bounds of divine revelation. And it is not useless to show in examples into what monstrous and blasphemous opinions those have fallen who, without, beyond, and outside the Word of God, have followed their thoughts on the image of the human mind in the matter of the Trinity. As we read those things in Irenaeus, book 2, we cannot but shudder. It can also be seen in Tatian's *Oration*

---

* A Gnostic heretic who lived in Alexandria, Egypt and taught from A.D. 117 to 138.

against the Greeks* and in Philo's *On the Creation of the World***, that from those speculations without and beyond the Word, the doctrine of the Trinity was corrupted. Similar things are also recounted by Athanasius in the *Oration* against the followers of Sabellius, which is useful to examine. Therefore, if the purity of doctrine in this article is maintained, and those ancient images and likenesses are reverently and piously used only for the sake of explanation and kept within the limits of the Word, we have no reason to disturb the Church with agitations and quibbles about these likenesses.

---

* Tatian wrote his apologetic work, *Oratio ad Graecos*, sometime between A.D. 155 and 165. Tatian became a member of the ascetic Encratite sect.
** Philo (B.C 40 to A.D. 20) wrote *On the Creation* as an allegorical interpretation of Genesis.

III.
On Free Will.*

The controversies concerning this article are neither idle quibbles nor disputes, but as LUTHER rightly judged, the purity of the doctrine of the Law concerning the corruption and depravity of human powers through the fall, as well as the Gospel concerning the benefits of the Son of God, cannot be retained in the Church unless the topic of free will [*libero arbitrio*] is vindicated from all corruptions according to the Word of God. Nor would it be difficult to show, from Justin, Irenaeus, Tertullian, Clement, Origen, and Chrysostom, that the principal points of Christian doctrine concerning sin and justification were either corrupted or at least miserably obscured, chiefly because the doctrine of free will was diverted from the standard of the Word of God to natural reasoning [*cogitationes physicas*], and that the restoration of some light on the doctrine of grace, began by the grace of God, in the time of Augustine, with the purification of the doctrine on free will.

In the same way, through the ministry of LUTHER, God began the restoration of purer doctrine from the Word of God by clarifying this issue. And there is no doubt that if any obscurities are again allowed into this matter, the purity of the doctrine, which, by the immense grace of God and through the ministry of LUTHER, has been most clearly illuminated from the Word of God, will once again be enveloped in darkness. I say this so that this controversy is not dismissed among idle and unnecessary disputes, but rather that its judgment, true, clear, and transparent, pleasing to God and beneficial to the Church, may be drawn from Scripture and handed down to posterity.

---

* This chapter anticipates Formula of Concord Article II Epitome and Solid Declaration, "Concerning the Free Will and Human Powers."

Many questions are connected to this issue which need to be distinguished to avoid confusion. Indeed, the division by the ancients is learned, which states that there are four questions regarding human free will: 1. before the Fall, 2. after the Fall but before restoration, 3. after renewal but before glorification, and 4. in the state of glorification itself. But since there are no current disputes regarding the first and fourth stages, we will only present those questions that have raised controversies in recent times and require explanation and resolution.*

The question of the cause of sin: LUTHER foresaw the debates about this question, writing in [his commentary on] Genesis chapter 26 with these words: "I wanted to caution and instruct diligently and precisely because, after my death, many will bring out my books and from them will confirm all sorts of errors and delusions of their own. Among other things, I wrote that all things are absolute and necessary, but I also added that we must look to the revealed God. But they will skip all those parts and only take up those about the hidden God. So, you who hear me now, remember that I taught not to inquire into the predestination of the hidden God, but to rest in what is revealed through the calling and ministry of the Word." These are LUTHER's words. And already there are whispers here and there that everything happens by absolute necessity. Also, that God works all things, both good and evil deeds, in men. And although these ideas are currently suppressed, there is no doubt that they will eventually burst forth openly. Furthermore, debates about the coercion of the unregenerate will are being openly raised.

Therefore, it is necessary to oppose the reckless spirits and hand down to posterity a single, true, correct, and clarified opinion, which is in accordance with faith, pleasing to God, and beneficial

---

* See Epitome II:1. In the Epitome, the topic is further narrowed to "primary question" being the second one.

and salutary for consciences, so that from those opinions found in the early writings of LUTHER* and Philip [Melanchthon]**, new and absurd disputes are not stirred up, just as Eck did in Augsburg and Regensburg, agitating those discussions from the early writings of LUTHER and Philip for entire days. It is also useful to retain the form and doctrine, and the words that are found in the 19th Article of the Augsburg Confession, and to understand how almost every word is opposed to such disputes, I will distribute it in the following way.

1. When we contemplate the providence of God sustaining nature, and God's foreknowledge, which cannot err; also, the fact that nothing can happen without God's will; and that God ordains the course of events, not the other way around, we encounter many inscrutable matters, and it seems to lead to the absolute necessity of everything, whether in good or evil actions. But LUTHER refers to these speculations as concerning "the hidden God." And in [his commentary on] Genesis 17, he says, "As for the unknown God, that is, not revealed through His Word, what He is, what He does, what He wants, are none of my concern. What concerns me is to know what He has commanded, what He has promised, what He has threatened." Therefore, in this matter, our beliefs and statements should not be based on speculations and deductions about the hidden and unknown God, but according to God's revealed Word.

2. It must be explicitly stated as a negative: That God is not the author, or cause, of sin. And this proposition must be explained: That God did not create sin in the beginning; and that now in this corrupted nature, He neither desires, approves, assists, nor works sin; nor does He compel anyone to sin.

---

* e.g. *De servo arbitrio*, i.e. *The Bondage of the Will* (1525). It should be noted that even when Chemnitz cites Luther referring to the "hidden God," he does not cite *The Bondage of the Will*, but instead relies on a later work.
** e.g., *Loci Communes* (1521).

3. Yet sinners are not thereby completely exempted from the command, providence, and governance of God. For the determination of God has decreed the limits to which He will allow sin to go—when and where He will restrain the wicked. He also thwarts and overturns many plans, represses many efforts, and diverts them for other purposes, either for the sake of the Church or so that the wicked may bring destruction upon themselves. Often He even turns the worst schemes and attempts of the wicked to the good of the Church, as Joseph says in Genesis 45:8. Sometimes, God uses the malice stirred up by the devil and arising from the will of the wicked themselves to inflict deserved punishments on those whom He chooses to visit in His judgment, as with Shimei in 2 Samuel 16:5 and following. Finally, sins are often the punishments of sins by the just judgment of God. Scripture often uses active verbs when speaking of this topic in this sense. And although we cannot fully discern this mysterious governance of God, we must reverently hold to this axiom: "God is not the author of sin."

4. An affirmative must also be added, namely, that the cause of sin is the will of the devil and the wicked. The devil is the cause of sin not only because he has been sinning from the beginning (John 8:44), nor merely because through the devil's envy sin entered the world through one man (Wisdom 2:24, Romans 5:12); but because he is effective in the children of unbelief (Ephesians 2:2). Whoever commits sin is of the devil (1 John 3:8). He blinds minds (2 Corinthians 4:4), fills the heart (Acts 5:3), and holds people captive to do his will (2 Timothy 2:26). However, lest the wicked seek a pretext for excuse from this tyranny, as if they were forced against their will to commit crimes and therefore are worthy of pardon rather than punishment, James points out the proximate cause of sin: "Each person is tempted when they are dragged away by their own evil desire and enticed. Then, after desire has conceived, it gives birth to sin" (James 1:14–15). Therefore, in the

article of the [Augsburg] Confession, the will of the devil and of wicked men are joined.

Therefore, the debate about the coercion of the unregenerate will must be rejected because it diminishes original sin as if it were not a corruption in the mind and obstinacy in the will, but only a penalty of coercion. Also, it absolves the wicked—if not entirely, then to a great extent, as the schools say—and thereby it transfers the cause of sin from the mind and will to the will of the devil. However, original sin and the tyranny of the devil consist in this: Not that in the unregenerate, the mind being ignorant, the will being forced, unwilling, and resisting, as if they were being compelled to crimes with a twisted neck, but because nature is so corrupted by original sin that, blinded and bewitched by the deceits of the devil, it makes itself compliant in all its directions, with mind, will, and affections. Thus, speaks James in 1:14 and Proverbs 2:13. They [the unregenerate] rejoice in the most harmful things. Indeed, about those who are given over to a reprobate mind, the Scripture says in Romans 1:24, "God gave them over in the sinful desires of their hearts." Psalm 81:13 says, "I gave them over to the stubbornness of their hearts." And in Ephesians 2:3, where the tyranny of the devil is described, it expressly names the desires and the will of the flesh and thoughts. For this is attributed only to the regenerate in Romans 7:15, "For what I do not want to do, this I keep on doing," and Galatians 5:17, "so that you are not to do whatever you want."

So Augustine, in his work, *Against Two Letters of the Pelagians*, book 1, chapter 10, states, "Free will in a sinner has not been lost to such an extent that it is through this free will that most people sin, especially those who sin with pleasure and love for sin, because what pleases them is what they desire." He also says, "This will, which is free in evil acts, is therefore not free in good acts, because it has not been liberated." And again, "They have free will in evil, to which the pleasure of malice has been joined by sin, either more secretly or more openly, or the individual has persuaded themselves of it." In this sense, and for this reason, when the early Church Fathers say that a person has free will in evil, or that the unregenerate free will is capable of sinning, Augustine explains in book 2 of *On Grace and Free Will*: "Let no one accuse God in their heart, but let each person blame themselves when they sin." That is, the cause of sin should not be attributed to anything else, but should be recognized within oneself: In one's mind, will, heart, and desires.

This relates to the distinction made by Damascene* and Bernard**: There is one kind of necessity, *the necessity of coercion*, where the principle or cause is external to the person, such that the individual contributes nothing to it and strongly resists throughout the entire coercion. Bernard rightly says that this necessity does not apply to the will. Augustine considers it as absurd to say that the will is forced by necessity as to say that something hot lacks heat. And LUTHER states, "If the will is forced, it is not will, but constraint." [*Voluntas si cogatur, non est voluntas, sed noluntas.*] There is another kind of necessity, *the necessity of immutability*, where a person willingly chooses and acts on something, but cannot choose between two opposites and is immutably bound to one side only. Augustine correctly attributes this necessity to the unregenerate will. For, as Bernard says, it does not have equal power and ease between good and evil; instead, it is so corrupted by sin that it can only think of sin, choose sin, and delight in sin. Bernard beautifully explains this in his *Sermons on the Song of Songs*, Sermon 81: "In some perverse and strange way, the will itself, having been changed

---

* John of Damascus (676–749), a notable theologian often cited in Chemnitz's works on Christology.
** Bernard of Clairvaux (1090–1153), a significant medieval theologian and monastic reformer of the Western Church, who was often affirmatively cited by Luther and other Reformation theologians.

for the worse by sin, creates a necessity, such that this necessity, being voluntary, cannot excuse the will, nor can the will, being enticed, exclude necessity. For this necessity is in some way voluntary; it is a kind of force that flatters by pressing and presses by flattering. Hence that voice complains, as if groaning under the burden of this necessity, 'Lord, I suffer violence, answer for me.' But knowing again that he can not justly blame the Lord, since his own will was more to blame, he confidently added, 'What shall I say, or how shall I answer, when I myself am at fault?' Thus, he was pressed by a yoke, but it was none other than that of a certain voluntary servitude, and he was indeed miserable as a servant, but inexcusable as a willing participant. For it was the will that made itself a servant of sin by consenting to sin, and it is still the will that remains under sin by serving it willingly." So says Bernard. Augustine has a similar sentiment in the 8th book of his *Confessions*, chapter 5.

The essence of the argument is this: The concept of free will in matters of evil must be asserted in such a way that neither the doctrine of original sin nor the tyranny of the devil is diminished or obscured. Conversely, the tyranny of the devil over the unregenerate, according to Scripture, must be so emphasized that the will of the wicked is not absolved of blame and the cause of sin is not shifted to the punishment of coercion. Moreover, discussions about necessity must be conducted in such a manner that we do not make God the author and cause of sin. If this standard is maintained, discerning these issues is not difficult.

IV.
On External Discipline or the Righteousness of the Flesh.

Regarding external discipline or the righteousness of the flesh, the opinion expressed in the Augsburg Confession and its Apology should be maintained. These texts discuss the extent of freedom the unregenerate man's will has in external matters and actions and how far it can progress in obeying God's commands. The foundational principles that give rise to this limited freedom in external disciplines of reason must also be retained. Although in these rational exercises the inner movements may either be absent or not in agreement, the question at hand is what the unregenerate mind, without the Holy Spirit, can understand and judge; what the will can choose; and what the external members can accomplish under restraint. Paul attributes to Pharisaic righteousness not only external actions and a certain appearance devoid of any internal movement, but also, in Romans 9:31, he says they pursue a law of righteousness, and in Romans 10:3, they seek to establish their own righteousness. He also acknowledges their zeal for God in Romans 10:2, Philippians 3:6, and Galatians 1:6. Regarding the Gentiles, he speaks in Romans 1 and 2 in such a way as to clearly describe some internal movements in the mind and will. He credits the unregenerate Gentiles with the righteousness of the Law, which they inherently possess, stating that the work of the Law is written in their hearts and that what can be known about God is evident within them. He refers to the syllogistic reasoning that can somewhat deduce the invisible attributes of God from the works of creation, and [demonstrates] that by nature they can perform the works of the Law. These points are clear, and as Augustine says, the sheer evidence should be convincing enough without the need for lengthy arguments.

Therefore, it is sheer recklessness to undermine the common understanding of natural principles and knowledge. LUTHER has a clear opinion on this in [his commentary on] chapter 17 of Genesis, page 213: "By natural instinct, even the nations possess the understanding that there is some supreme deity that should be worshiped, invoked, and praised, and to which one should flee in all dangers, as Paul says in Romans 1:19 and 20, that the Gentiles recognized God by nature. This knowledge is divinely implanted in the minds of all men, who call upon God as a helper, beneficent and appeasable, although they later err in who that God is and how He wishes to be worshiped." This is what LUTHER says.

Because the question is not only about economic and political deeds, it is useful and necessary to clarify what this discipline of reason can achieve and how far it can progress in mind, will, and external actions when it has the Law of God and the Gospel as its object. And regarding the Law, it is certain that in this corrupt nature, the natural knowledge of the Law is by no means as clear and perfect as it was in uncorrupted nature before the fall. Also, there is a significant difference between what is said about the non-regenerate in Romans 2:15, "They show that the work of the law is written on their hearts," and what God says about the regenerate in Jeremiah 31:33, "I will put My Law in their hearts."

However, some light is added to this explanation if it is distributed in such a way that it is said to concern: 1. the knowledge of the Law; 2. the use of the Law; and, 3. the works of the Law.

1. Therefore, as far as the knowledge of the Law is concerned, reason knows only a part of the Law and understands it to some extent. However, [it knows nothing of] what it means for the Law to be spiritual, that is, to require spiritual movements and not to be satisfied with partial and external obedience but to demand

conformity of all the powers of the whole nature with the will of God, so that there should be no opposing desire, and that it demands this to the extent that whoever offends in one point is guilty of all, even if they maintain external discipline. Also, that the depravity of nature and natural lawlessness is sin, which reason does not know or understand (Romans 7:7). Also, what it truly means to fear God, to love God, to believe God, and that all works must proceed from true faith, fear, and love of God, and be oriented to this end of offering worship and obedience to God, is not written in the natural knowledge as it is now. And concerning the threats of God's wrath, Moses himself says in Psalm 90:11, "Who knows the power of your anger?" Even the natural knowledge itself is said by Paul to be corrupted in various ways in the unregenerate. Romans 1:21, "They became futile in their thoughts." Also in verse 28, "And even as they did not like to retain God in their knowledge, God gave them over to a debased mind, to do those things which are not fitting." And in these very natural notions of the Law, the assent is often weak or non-existent. Often, the emotions rebel against the judgment of the mind, as Paul describes callousness in Ephesians 4:19. These demonstrate the original corruption even in the righteousness of the flesh.

2. Regarding the use of the Law, reason somewhat understands its political [i.e., civil] use; however, concerning the spiritual and theological use of the Law, reason knows nothing at all.* This is because God demands perfect obedience in the Law not because we can fulfill it, but so that, feeling our weakness, we may recognize that we cannot be justified by our works. Also, the Law works wrath not because God desires the death of the sinner, but to serve as a tutor leading to Christ. Therefore, reason, on its own without

---

* Chemnitz's argument is essentially a reiteration and amplification of Article XIX of the Apology, especially ¶9, where the distinction between civil and spiritual righteousness is clearly articulated.

the Holy Spirit, from the doctrine of the Law either becomes hypocritical, presuming on its own strength and righteousness; or it becomes complacent, because it does not know the power of God's wrath, as stated in Psalm 90:11, or it despairs, because it does not understand that the Law is a tutor leading to Christ.

3. Regarding the works of the Law, indeed, the Gentiles naturally perform the external disciplines of the Law, as stated in Romans 2:14. But the spiritual works of the Law are utterly impossible for reason, in terms of the efficient cause, the formal cause, and the final cause, such as to truly recognize and detest sin through genuine repentance, to truly and correctly fear God's wrath, to desire against the flesh, to mortify the old man, and to choose, initiate, and perform other spiritual movements which the Law speaks of, in both tables [of the Decalogue]. For these are the works and benefits of the Spirit of renewal, who writes the Law in the hearts of believers and makes them walk in His commandments. Thus, what Paul says in 2 Corinthians 3:15 remains true: When Moses is read, a veil lies on their heart, and it is not removed except through the Spirit of freedom.

From this, it is clear what the discipline of reason can achieve and how far it can progress when it is faced with the Law of God, and what distinguishes the discipline of reason from the gifts or operations of the Holy Spirit. And from these sources, many paradoxes of the Scholastics are refuted.

In the same way, it must be explained what and how much the discipline of reason can achieve when its object is the Gospel. And because the Gospel is a mystery hidden for ages, which not even the princes—that is, the most distinguished of this age—have known, reason has no natural knowledge of the Gospel's doctrine, as it does of the Law. However, as Augustine[*] says in *De Fide ad*

---

[*] Often incorrectly attributed to Augustine, this work was actually written by Fulgentius of Ruspe (A.D. 462–527).

Petrum, it can read the words of the Gospel or hear them from the preacher, discuss their meaning and sense, and to some extent even understand the words, as is evident among the Jews, and indeed to conceive a historical faith*, as LUTHER speaks of acquired faith. For this [that is, historical faith] is also attributed to the devil himself in James 2:19, and is evident in many enemies of the Gospel. But the true meaning and use of the Gospel, in true exercises, reason not only does not understand from reading and hearing, but it completely perverts it. Either it hates and persecutes the Gospel because it thinks that this doctrine harms good morals; or it conjures up the notion that God does not care about sin, and that the threats of God's wrath are a myth; or it judges that the promise of grace does not pertain to itself, nor can it establish in temptations that grace abounds over sin; or under the guise of an external profession, it thinks that it can be saved by the Gospel without conversion (for they believe this to be the message of the Gospel, that those who do not renounce the external profession of the Gospel are saved without conversion). Paul calls this a veiled or covered Gospel in 2 Corinthians 4:3. Therefore, the true understanding, true assent, and application of the Gospel promise are not the work of reason; rather, they are gifts and operations of the Holy Spirit.

And so remains what Paul says, 1 Cor. 2:14, "The natural man does not receive the things of the Spirit of God." He calls such a person ψυχικός, that is, one who does not have the Spirit of God, as the Epistle of Jude says in verse 19. [By this,] he does not refer to someone who is without reason, a swine from the herd of Epicurus, such as those in 2 Pet. 2:12, who are called irrational animals, but because the most significant part of a man, namely the soul, whose faculties are the mind and will, excels and is strong, whom 1 Cor. 2:6 calls the rulers of this age. About such a man, if he encounters

---

* That is, belief simply in the factual nature of events recorded in Scripture, which is defined in opposition to saving faith, which trusts in Jesus as the Christ.

the wisdom of God revealed through the Holy Spirit, he says two things: 1. ὁυ δυναται γνῶναι—He does not say that he does not *want* to understand, but instead, he *cannot* attain true knowledge either from reading or hearing the Gospel through the faculties of the natural man. And he adds the reason: Because the things of the Spirit of God are spiritually discerned. Here it is to be noted that true knowledge of God is a spiritual judgment, which is the true meaning of the Gospel, that is, as he himself explains, what is the mind of God and Christ. He denies this to the unregenerate man with quite harsh words: 2. he cannot recognize. ὁυ δέχεται [does not receive]. This word is used in Acts 8:14 in this way. Samaria received the Word of God (Acts 17:21). The Thessalonians received the Word of God with all eagerness, examining the Scriptures daily (1 The. 1:6). 1 The. 2:13, "You received it not as the word of men." Paul understands by this a firm assent, which establishes this as God's will, namely, to love the Word, delight in the meditation of Scripture, grasp and apply the promise to oneself. Paul denies that this acceptance (δέχεσθαι) can be provided by the faculties of the natural man. And he adds a reason: Because to such a man, the things of the Spirit of God are foolishness. And even if they see some sense in the words, since it is not approved by reason, assent is not given. And Paul does not only speak in the negative: "cannot" (ὁυ δυναται); but in 2 Corinthians 10:5, he says that the arguments of man's reason "exalt themselves against the knowledge of God," and therefore must be destroyed, and every thought must be taken captive to obey Christ. He says this is done by the power of God (2 Corinthians 10:8). As for spiritual motions of conversion to be conceived from hearing or reading the Gospel, it is clearly not within the capacity of the natural powers of the unregenerate man, as Paul says about thoughts in 2 Corinthians 3:5, about initiation in Philippians 1:6, and about the willingness and works in Philippians 2:13, as we will discuss later.

This distinction necessarily needs to be demonstrated when discussing the discipline that a non-regenerate person can provide.

Furthermore, in this context, it is also necessary to address the explanation of two questions that are currently being debated in a hazardous and ambiguous manner.

Although external discipline is not the initiation of spiritual movements, nor does it satisfy the commands of God, and thus neither merits nor apprehends the grace of God (since God demands this discipline from all, even the non-regenerate, and punishes its violation in various ways) how is it [i.e., external discipline] (as the Augsburg Confession speaks) a pedagogy to Christ? Is it a preparation, a disposition, or the first approach to the grace of God? The Scholastics, when they discuss the merit of congruence, essentially mean this: A person who is without the Holy Spirit cannot indeed perform spiritual movements [that are] pleasing to God, or, as they themselves say, meritorious; however, it is congruent with the mercy of God that, when God sees a person doing as much as they can with the powers of free will concerning the object of the Law and the Gospel, God should work in such a person to bring about conversion.* Erasmus speaks thus: "The soul is prepared by external discipline and made more suitable to receive grace." Pighius says, "God gives His grace, but to those who have suitably disposed themselves with the works of free will." The opinion of Cassian, condemned among others by Prosper, was this: "When God sees us wanting to turn to good, He immediately rushes in, enlightens, directs, and strengthens." And indeed, the recent sentiment about repeated conversion echoes this: "When we do what is ours to do, then God also does what is His."

Those also do not speak correctly or adequately who say that the eunuch in Acts 8:27–28 achieved all those things by the powers

---

* See Formula of Concord, Solid Declaration, II:76.

of free will: That he went to Jerusalem to pray; that he read Isaiah in his chariot; [that he] recognized that he could not grasp the true meaning without an interpreter, pondered, desired the true understanding, and asked Philip for an explanation of the passage. (See the works of Wigand, part 2, pages 624 and 625.) Likewise, [they claim that] it was merely the discipline of reason from the powers of free will, without the Holy Spirit, that in Acts 10:2–3, 5 Cornelius was religious, feared God, fasted, distributed alms, and prayed to God, until an angel revealed to him that Peter was to be summoned. Because in Acts 8:29, seeing the eunuch's effort, the Spirit of the Lord instructed Philip to approach him. And, in Acts 10:4, the angel explicitly says, "Your prayers and your alms have ascended as a memorial before God," from this follows not only the disposition and preparation for grace through the discipline of reason, but the entire merit of congruence, which, observing those carnal efforts, God leads them to His grace, as LUTHER extensively discusses and explains in relation to Cornelius in chapter 3 of Galatians.

Since these debates have now been raised and are being discussed, it is necessary to seek the true opinion, and care must be taken not to slip back, silently or obscurely, to the foundations from which the merit of congruity was once constructed, as the splendor of political virtues, which are observed in *Ethics*, greatly disturbs judgment.

Therefore, the Scholastics, looking at the most beautiful endeavors of the unregenerate, established this axiom: "A person, from purely natural abilities, doing what is in them, is able not to commit mortal sin." And although it may not be truly good and spiritual work, nor (according to their opinion) merit due reward, yet neither should punishment be due to the honorable efforts of discipline. So, they invented a certain middle ground, which God might regard as a fitting disposition in granting grace. Thus, Erasmus says that although Socrates did not perform honorable discipline by faith, he did not sin as severely as if he had raped his sister or poisoned his mother.

The true response is this: Although not all sins are equal—as LUTHER also states concerning Genesis 17, "God finds us all sinners, although some are more cautious, moderate, and, so to speak, more secure than others"—it is essential to firmly hold onto these principles: Whatever is not from faith is sin, and in all unregenerate people, all sins are mortal. Thus, the Apology correctly states, "It is false that a person who performs the works of the commandments outside of grace does not sin, for human hearts without the Holy Spirit are impious."* A bad tree cannot bear good fruit, and without faith, it is impossible to please God. Therefore, the discipline cannot and should not be attributed with the merit of congruence, preparation, disposition, or whatever name it is called by, which God would look upon to bestow His grace. Indeed, God adorns discipline with physical rewards, as Augustine applies Matthew 6:2 to this: "They have received their reward." But the question of God's grace and spiritual gifts is different. The refutation of the merit of congruence is clear in the example of the blinding of the Jews in Romans 9:31 and 11:7: Israel, by pursuing a law of righteousness, did not attain to the Law. Also, what Israel sought, it did not obtain, but they were blinded. Thus, in Matthew 21:31, Christ says to the Pharisees, "The tax collectors and prostitutes will enter the kingdom of God ahead of you," because the sense of confidence and merit naturally adheres to discipline.

However, neither partiality nor favoritism are established by God. For the promise is universal, and people are to be admonished not to perform actions contrary to it. The issue at hand is that, when God touches or moves the hearts of the unregenerate through the hearing of the Word, this is attributed not to the preparations or dispositions of reason through discipline, but to

---

* Apology XVIII:72.

grace, which, as Augustine often says, is not grace if it is not given freely. And in the most distressing examples, many hear the Word and are not converted, many are hardened and blinded, as shown in Deu. 29:29, Isa. 6:9, Mat. 13:14, John 12:40, Acts 28:6. God demonstrates that the efficacy of the Word is not in our control, but is purely an act of grace, so that we recognize that benefit and gratefully praise God for it. These things, for very many reasons, must be declared simply and clearly, without ambiguity.

The second question concerns how one can distinguish the efforts of reason and the discipline of the flesh from the initial movements of the Spirit, which are the beginnings of conversion. This inquiry is not about engaging in pointless sophistry; rather, it seeks an explanation regarding a significant and essential matter.

For some who have fallen, before they are again converted through the grace of the Holy Spirit, it is said that they ought to strive for all holiness of morals and righteousness, to hear the Law, to meditate diligently on the Word of God, to remember the everlasting covenant made with God in Baptism, and to often recall that their sins have deserved the wrath of God and eternal damnation. They should also try to ponder Christ's redemption and mercy, as much as they can with their natural abilities; then, according to the Word of God, they should conduct themselves and converse with the pious. Finally, they should ask both individual pious people and the entire Church to pray for them. All these things are simply said to be mere efforts of the flesh and reason. But from this opinion follow many things that are not only absurd and false, but also very harmful to struggling consciences. For when the heart does not feel that Pauline πληροφορίαν [full assurance] in temptation, Rom. 8:38, but struggles with weakness, trying to sustain itself on the promise of faith, desiring faith, there always intrudes the thought, "Perhaps the efforts are carnal, because I do not feel fervent spiritual movements." And the φρόνημα [mindset] of the flesh is hostility towards God. Also, whatever is not from faith is sin. Certainly, I would not properly console such a conscience if I were to say as they do: "If you persist in this effort of reason, you should not doubt at all that God will eventually, even in the very struggle, through the Word and the Holy Spirit, become effective, so that spiritual movements finally occur." This opinion posits many falsehoods: 1. As if there is a divine promise in that Scholastic axiom: "God unfailingly grants grace to the person who does what is in his power." 2. It makes carnal efforts the beginnings after which spiritual conversion and the Spirit's effectiveness must undoubtedly follow. 3. It leaves struggling and fearful consciences without the consolation of the Holy Spirit's presence, until the moment of death, even if it starts from the Word, unless they feel fervent spiritual movements. 4. It subtly suggests that the effectiveness of the Holy Spirit should be determined not from the Word, but from experience, when we feel spiritual movements, with such πληροφορία [full assurance] as described in Rom. 8:38.

How dangerously these things are debated can be judged by those who have either experienced it themselves or have seen the struggle of a tormented conscience in others due to the weakness of spiritual movements. For such thoughts disturb the weakness of faith on their own. There is no thought that the Holy Spirit is present with you and helping your weakness. Such thoughts, such efforts, as are found in you, often arise more strongly from flesh and reason, and whatever is without the Holy Spirit and not from faith is sin.

Indeed, this matter is of great and necessary concern. It is well known that this distinction exists: To the truly pious, the Holy Spirit sometimes seals His presence and efficacy with such a testimony that their hearts seem to burn with new movements, and they do not doubt His presence. However, sometimes this presence and efficacy of the Spirit is so hidden and overwhelmed by the cross or great weakness, that even great saints cry out, "Why have You abandoned me? And why have You forsaken me?" Here, we must not make the distinction that we should only believe we are sustained and governed by the Spirit of God when we feel the burning movements of the Spirit overpowering the weakness of the flesh. When we do not clearly feel the efficacy of the Spirit, but start from the Word with such weakness and often struggle, and the efforts of the flesh and reason seem more prominent, it may appear that the presence and efficacy of the Holy Spirit are lacking, and that the struggle is merely a struggle of the flesh. For the Scripture says that the power of God's grace is made perfect in weakness (2 Corinthians 12:9). Sometimes a person may commit to the Word and struggle with their own weakness and sinful desires; they wish they could more firmly assent, mourn their frailty, and try to sustain themselves solely by the Word. These certainly are not works of the flesh, but without a doubt, they are the power of God being perfected in weakness. For to desire against the flesh is the work of the Spirit. And Augustine beautifully says in *De Correptione et Gratia*, chapter 6, "Even to desire grace is the beginning of grace." Likewise, Augustine's treatment of the examples of Cornelius (Acts 10) in Epistle 106, and Zacchaeus (Luke 19) in *De diversis quaestionibus ad Simplicianum*, book 1, question 2, demonstrates that these beginnings were not from the discipline of reason, but from preceding grace.

So we must keep to the principle that we should start with the Word of God, for the Holy Spirit is effective through this means. And at times, we begin with sound teaching, following the true meaning and application of both the Law and the Gospel. If, from hearing and thinking about the Word, some light appears in the heart and a struggle begins against doubt and other harmful affections, the heart holds a desire, wishing it could more strongly agree, and thus it is saddened by its weakness, that it is moved so weakly and coldly. Yet it does not want to forsake the Word but tries to uphold itself with the promise to agree with the Word, sighs within itself, and asks for prayers on its behalf. Likewise, when a baptized person, who previously ignored the Word, feels thoughts, desires, and impulses, we should not doubt that this is the effect of the Spirit through the Word, and we should pray that these beginnings of not fleshly, but spiritual, gifts be increased, according to the saying: "He who began a good work in us will bring it to completion." {Phi. 1:6}

Therefore, this rule must also be maintained: In theology, faith and assent do not begin with experience, so that we first feel the presence of the Spirit and then believe. Rather, faith and assent look to the Word and grasp it, although often not only external experience, but even internal feeling, resists. Afterwards, when it is God's good will, the feeling of consolation follows.

These rules are certain. For Scripture affirms both: 1. that the heard and contemplated voice of the Gospel is the administration of the Spirit; 2. that the promise of the Spirit is received through faith—not that faith is the work of reason and precedes the grace of the Holy Spirit, but that the efficacy of the Holy Spirit is begun and recognized through the Word in this way, when it initiates and stirs up faith in the hearts of the hearers. It is certain that faith is recognition in the mind and assent in the will, which is not idle but resists the darkness or doubt in the mind, and distrust or complacency in the will. It is also certain that faith is not immediately or always complete and perfect in all aspects, but its beginnings are often very obscure and weak, and are greatly opposed by profound weakness; hence it is rightly called a "smoldering wick."

Therefore, when from the heard or contemplated Word some light, or at least a spark, of true recognition and understanding shines forth in the mind and is implanted in the heart, or there arises a desire or some attempt at assent, from which struggle ensues with doubt in the mind and distrust in the will, it is certain that the beginnings of faith are present. And Paul says that the promise of the Spirit is received through faith, that is, from the hearing of the Word, not as if the Holy Spirit is given as a result of the work performed without a good motion of the user, as the Scholastics speak, but He exerts His efficacy in this way when He initiates the beginnings of faith from the hearing of the Word, as has been said. These are simple, true, and salutary teachings, the correct explanation of which is necessary to be present in the Church.

V.
On the Capacity of the Unregenerate Free Will to Initiate and Accomplish Spiritual Motions in Conversion or Renewal.*

Therefore, it must be distinctly and clearly established what is the κρινόμενον [judged matter], or what is the status in this question.

The question now among us is not whether a man, without the Holy Spirit, by the powers of corrupted nature alone, can fulfill the law with perfect obedience and merit the forgiveness of sins and eternal life, as the Scholastics argue.**

Nor is the status of the controversy (as the controversies currently stand) sufficiently explained when it is said, "With the help of the Holy Spirit, the human will can initiate and effectuate spiritual motions." For even Pelagius formerly shrouded himself with this generality. Augustine, *Against Two Letters of the Pelagians*, in book 2, chapter 19, cites these words of Pelagius: "In every good work, man is assisted by grace." And in book 4, chapter 6, he cites this statement of Pelagius: "Grace assists the good intention of each person; however, it does not infuse the pursuit of virtue into those who resist, nor does it inspire a desire for good into those who are unwilling." Augustine says: "I would accept these without hesitation if they were not said by those [Pelagians], whose sentiment is known." For Pelagius understood these propositions as Augustine recounts his explanations: "Men by their own powers can wish, desire, and seek the grace of conversion. And when the will of desir-

---

* This chapter is also concerned with the issues addressed in FC II, Epitome and Solid Declaration.

** See FC Epitome II:9–10.

ing proceeds from free will, then the Holy Spirit is given to those asking." So far Pelagius. Also, Augustine says, "You say that man is assisted by grace in a good work, as though he began by himself, and is then helped in that very first work." Even the more sensible Scholastics say that free will is not enough to bring about spiritual actions unless it is helped by the Holy Spirit. The Pontificians [i.e., Papists] also now loudly proclaim the assistance of the Holy Spirit. Therefore, these statements are not sufficiently clear.

The status of this controversy is also not clearly defined when it is said without sufficient explanation that the human will behaves purely passively in conversion.* LUTHER indeed spoke correctly in that sense, which he piously explained. But many interweave Enthusiast opinions, as if conversion happens without any movement or change in the mind and will, as if we could freely resist the word and indulge in sinful desires, without any movement or change in the mind and will, without meditation, effort, and struggle, until we feel that conversion has been completed by the operation of the Holy Spirit. By these arguments, the controversy is entangled and obscured on both sides.

Therefore, let the issue or point of contention that is currently debated be explained in simple, clear, unambiguous, familiar, and widely understood terms, namely, since conversion is a change in the mind, will, and human powers, it is certain that in conversion there should be meditation on the Word, some recognition and understanding, an effort of assent, sighing, longing, and struggle with doubt and distrust. And, in summary, there must be some application of the mind and will to the grace of the Spirit, so that there is some resistance. Where there is no change in the mind and will, no meditation, recognition, effort, desire, or struggle, but the whole mind and will entirely resist and put forth the opposite action; in short, where there is no application whatsoever, there,

---

* See FC Epitome II:18

beyond dispute, neither is conversion nor can there be. And if some understand the purely passive state in conversion in this way, they are clearly and dangerously mistaken.

Therefore, the issue at hand is not whether the things we mentioned occur and should be present in conversion, but whether the mind and will in conversion have, from the natural powers of the old man's free will, the ability to perform the actions or movements we have mentioned, or whether these are gifts and workings of the renewing Spirit in the new man, who is created in the image of God in conversion, as the Scripture speaks. And to avoid any deception hidden by ambiguity when it is answered that this happens with the help of the Holy Spirit, it must be explicitly asked whether the non-regenerated will, before conversion, has any capacity whatsoever from the natural powers of the old man, which, although so weak that it cannot of itself proceed to action or bring about conversion or spiritual movements, can still do something very small if aided by the Holy Spirit; that is, can it cooperate from itself and from the old nature to some extent, so that when the Holy Spirit offers His grace and efficacy, can the non-regenerated will from the natural powers of the old man apply itself to grace, attempt, assent, struggle, not resist? Moreover, the notion that the Augsburg Confession [*Chimaera Augustana*] claims that this natural faculty of the old, unregenerated will, as if it were sleeping and snoring, can still be awakened by the Holy Spirit is fanciful.*

When the issue of controversy is set forth in this manner, as it truly is, then unless we wish to reject and deny many and very clear sentences of Scripture, the response is easy and straightforward.

And it is a useful observation that regarding this question, many fathers were led astray by the thoughts of physical reasons, and thus have erred. Chrysostom says in homily 52 on Genesis,

---

* The point that Chemnitz is making is that heretics were claiming that the Augsburg Confession taught this false doctrine, an assertion contrary to fact.

"Just as without assistance, we can do nothing right; so, unless we attribute what is ours, we cannot acquire divine favor." Augustine writes that some argued this way in Gaul: "In the unregenerate will, there remains such a capability that by its natural effort it can seek a healer, desire conversion, begin." And they added: "Unless such a capability is attributed to the unregenerate will, God cannot be defended from partiality." The Scholastics quote from the book *On Ecclesiastical Dogmas**, "We have the beginning of our salvation by God's mercy, but to acquiesce to the saving inspiration is within our power." And Augustine himself admits in *On Predestination*, chapter 3, that he once held the [same] opinion: "I said," he says, "it is ours to believe and to will, but God's to endow those believing and willing with the ability."

Also, he confesses to have thought that the grace of God consists only in that the will of God is revealed to us in the Gospel, but that to consent to the preached Gospel is our own and from ourselves. Also, there are passages in *On the Spirit and the Letter*, chapters 33 and 34, where he argues at length that it is of one's own will to consent to God's call.

But he [Augustine] retracts and refutes this opinion in chapter 3 of *On the Predestination of the Saints* and adds that he was moved when he looked more closely at the doctrine of original sin. Also, these passages, 2 Cor. 3:5: "Not that we are sufficient of ourselves"; Phi. 1:6: "It is God who works in you, both to will and to work for His good pleasure"; John 15:5: "Without Me you can do nothing"; 1 Cor. 4:7: "What do you have that you did not receive?" Taught by these and similar testimonies of Scripture, Augustine later embraced and strongly defended this opinion: Holy thought, good intention, and the desire for good do not begin or

---

* *De Ecclesiasticis Dogmatibus* was once falsely attributed to St. Augustine of Hippo. In reality, it was a work of a Semi-Pelagian, Gennadius of Marseilles (d. 496).

emerge from the powers of the unregenerate will but are grace, a gift, and the operation of the Holy Spirit. And for the purpose of teaching, first, he calls this grace "prevenient," that is, preceding or antecedent. Then, second, that we may acquiesce to the inspiration of the Holy Spirit, assent, or at least try to assent, and not resist but struggle against concupiscence, he confirms that this is not a capacity of the unregenerate will, but is grace, a gift, and the operation of the Holy Spirit. He calls this grace "preparatory." Thirdly, he also proves that when desire and good intention are present, it is not in our power to change the will for the better, but God works to will (Phi. 2:13), and removes the heart of stone (Eze. 36:26). He calls this grace "operative," and he distinguishes it from what he calls "co-operative" grace because it is solely God's work to remove the heart of stone and to give a new heart. Augustine has many most elegant sentences, which are noted elsewhere.

Although Augustine had fortified this true opinion with the strongest testimonies of Scripture, nevertheless it seemed too harsh to posterity. Therefore, "moderations" were sought (as is known from histories) by Cassian[*], Hesychius[**], Gennadius[***], Faustus[****], Hormisdas[*****], etc. However, the testimonies by which this opinion is shown to be most firm and is confirmed and different opinions are refuted, we have noted elsewhere.

Augustine has the most beautiful sentences of this kind, including *On Grace and Free Will*, chapter 16: "It is certain that we will when we want, but He makes us want, who works in us to will.

---

[*] John Cassian (A.D. 360–435), a mystic who had a substantial influence on the form of Western monasticism.
[**] Hesychius of Jerusalem (d. A.D. 450).
[***] Again, Gennadius of Marseilles.
[****] Faustus of Riez (ca. A.D. 400–490), a bishop in southern Gaul. One of his works was condemned for semi-Pelagianism at the Synod of Orange (A.D. 529).
[*****] Pope Hormisdas (A.D. 450–523), who refused to condemn Faustus of Riez.

It is also certain that we do when we act; but He makes us act, who works in us to accomplish." From *Correction and Grace*, chapter 2: "They understand, if they are children of God, that they are driven by the Spirit of God, so that they may do what must be done; and when they have done it, they give thanks to Him by whom they are driven. For they are driven in order that they may act, not so that they themselves do nothing." And from *On Ecclesiastical Dogmas*, chapter 32: "God acts in us so that we may will and act, and He does not allow to be idle in us the gifts that are to be exercised, not neglected."

Because conversion, in all its parts, is not completed at once or in a single moment, it should not be said that the will must be idle and purely passive until it feels the conversion to be complete.* Nor, because conversion and renewal are the work of God, should faith not care whether it happens or has happened; rather, it should be entrusted to God, who will be able to accomplish His work. Such were the circumstances of Augustine, which led him to write treatises on grace and free will, and also on correction and grace. But as the initial stages of conversion are given to us by the Holy Spirit, immediately arises the struggle of flesh and Spirit, which clearly happens not without the movement of our will. And this cooperation of the will, not the old [will], but the one that began to be renewed, and those beginnings in great weakness grow and increase, not without the movement of our will. And so it is correctly said: "Grace leading, the will following." However, this cooperation always depends on the grace of God; without it, even the gifts cease and are lost, as Augustine beautifully says in *Correction and Grace*, chapter 12: "If those reborn were left in such weakness that they could remain in God's help if they wished, and God did not work in them to will, their will would succumb to their weakness amid

---

* See FC Solid Declaration II:59.

so many and such great temptations. Therefore, the weakness of the human will was helped so that divine grace would act inseparably, and, therefore, although weak, it would not succumb."

The remaining things which belong here against the Enthusiasts also concerning cooperating grace, and why the freedom of the new creature must be impressed; also that the instrument or medium through which the Holy Spirit begins and operates the first motion or impulse of the will, are noted in the place concerning free will.*

For "Whether the grace of the Holy Spirit is given to those who resist" must be clearly explained. However, we have already said before that Pelagius once played with the ambiguity of that question. But if it is understood that the Holy Spirit is given to those who do not resist, that is, to those who by the effort of reason and the powers of the old free will, before the operation of the Spirit, have acquired for themselves the good will, the desire, or who have such a nature that it is of itself obedient to the Holy Spirit, then the opinion is clearly false and Pelagian. For the Holy Spirit is given to us whose nature of itself is such that, as the Scripture says, it is dead in trespasses, free from righteousness, a slave to sin, whose heart's imagination is evil, the wisdom of the flesh that is enmity against God, which is not subject to the Law of God, nor can be. However, the Holy Spirit is given not so that we may freely indulge in resistance, so to speak, but so that the unwilling may become willing and the resistant may become unresistant. Where there is no struggle against that resistance, but it is freely indulged, there it is certain that there is no grace of the Holy Spirit, no conversion.

However, if this question ("Whether the Holy Spirit is given to those who resist") is understood to be about those who, when the Holy Spirit is working, giving, and bestowing that grace to the

---
* FC Epitome II:19.

mind and will, so that they can think, desire, attempt, struggle, assent, comply, completely resist, and with the opposite act dissolve the work of the Holy Spirit, then it is rightly and truly said, "The grace of the Holy Spirit is not given to those who resist."

Just as a man in conversion and afterwards is divided into new and old, so two things happen in conversion in this whole life: 1. [Man] takes delight in the Law of God, and the will is present within him (Rom. 7:22), from Him who works to will (Phi. 2:13), who makes us think something good (2 Cor. 3:5). The Spirit desires against the flesh (Gal. 5:17). It struggles with weakness and tries to assent. 2. The flesh desires against the Spirit (Gal. 5:17). The Law in us not only rebels against the law of the mind, but also takes it captive (Rom. 7:21) and is enmity against God (Rom. 8:7). The former is a gift and work of the Holy Spirit in the new man; the latter is the operation and efficacy of the natural free will, from the powers of the old man.

Therefore, if it is asked what the free will of the old man does and operates from its natural powers in conversion, it is correctly answered that it not only behaves as a passive subject, but also resists, rebels, and is hostile against the grace of God. However, in conversion, the old Adam is put to death, and the body of sin is destroyed (Rom. 6:6, and 2 Cor. 4:16). The outer man is decaying, and the inner man is being renewed day by day. Therefore, the resistance of the old man in conversion and after conversion is not entirely the same as it is before conversion, for it is put to death and destroyed.*

---

* See FC Solid Declaration II:67

VI.
On the Definition of the Gospel.*

The head and foundation of the doctrine of Justification is to rightly discern between the Law and the Gospel, and to clearly establish from the true foundations of Scripture what the proper doctrine of the Gospel is, which must be distinguished from the Law insofar as it preaches about the benefits of the Son of God as Mediator, and reveals the righteousness of faith before God. For at all times, many harmful illusions in the article of Justification have occurred because the proper doctrine of the Gospel, in which righteousness before God is revealed, was not correctly established. And this was the occasion for many errors, because, just as the Law is defined in the Prophetic books, so the Gospel was defined in the Apostolic writings. To say nothing of the gross dreams of the Scholastics about the old and new law, even Augustine argues in *On Faith and Works*, chapter 9, that the proper doctrine of the Gospel concerns not only faith but also the morals of the faithful. In book 1 of *Preparation for the Gospel*, Eusebius makes a philosophical description, the essence of which is this: The doctrine of the Gospel teaches a religion by which souls are turned to God, to carry out His commands for life, from which arises friendship between God and men, and this life is blessedness. Jerome in the prologue to Mark says there are four qualities from which the holy Gospels are woven: *Precepts*, which command to avoid evil; *Commands*, which order to do good; *Testimonies*, which show what is to be believed about Christ; [and] *Examples*, which demonstrate perfection, as in "learn from Me."

These fathers and many others could not correctly convey the doctrine of Justification, or if they had any light, they could not

---
* See FC Epitome and Solid Declaration Article V, "On the Law and the Gospel."

be consistent. For this foundation is clear: The righteousness of God is revealed apart from the Law in the Gospel (Rom. 1:17 and 3:21). Therefore, if this is the proper doctrine of the Gospel, as they define it, it follows that the righteousness of faith not only consists in the application of the free promise of the forgiveness of sins for the sake of the Mediator, but also renewal, or good works, is substantial part.

This is well noted by the Papal adversaries, therefore they seek various distortions to confuse, obscure, and remove this necessary distinction concerning the proper doctrine of the Gospel, revealing the righteousness of faith before God, for they see then the path to be most direct. For if it is established that the proper doctrine of the Gospel is not only about the faith of the free promise for the sake of Christ, but also about renewal or good works, then it immediately follows that good works also enter into Justification as a partial cause, because in the Gospel the righteousness of God is revealed (Rom. 3:21). From this, the Cologne theologians* argue that in the definition of the Gospel, "teaching them to observe all that I have commanded you" (Mat. 28:20), that is, the commandments of charity should be added. Wicelius** contends that the works of the Law are different from good works, concerning which the Gospel preaches; and because the Gospel is the doctrine of Justification, good works are also required for Justification as a cause. Groperus***, however, plays quite deceitfully. Because the benefit of Christ is not only reconciliation but also sanctification, or renewal, and the Gospel, which reveals the righteousness of faith

---

* This categorization would include Gropper, and possibly Witzel.

** Georg Witzel (A.D. 1501–1573) was a Lutheran for a brief time before defecting to the Roman Church following the Diet of Augsburg in 1530.

*** Johann Gropper (A.D. 1503–1559) a Papist of Erasmian inclinations, was involved with numerous colloquies with the Lutherans. In the years of the Augsburg Interim, Gropper functioned as an imperial commissioner. Although well-received by the papacy and offered the chance to become a cardinal (which he declined), he was later denounced to the Inquisition and died in poverty.

before God, preaches about the whole benefit of Christ, the righteousness of faith consists of and is completed by these two parts, namely the forgiveness of sins and the internal renewal of the will, from which good works are produced as fruits.

I mention these things so that it may be considered that dealing with this foundation, namely, what the proper doctrine of the Gospel is, in which the righteousness of God is revealed from faith for faith (Rom. 1:17) is not idle quibbling. For it is impossible to retain the purity of the article on the doctrine of Justification if delusion is admitted in this foundation, as we have shown with examples.

Paul explicitly says that in the Gospel the righteousness of God is revealed apart from the Law; therefore, the main point in this question is to establish and diligently maintain the true and clear distinction between the doctrine of the Law and the Gospel. And LUTHER truly and elegantly says in [his 1535 commentary on] chapter 2 of Galatians, "He who knows well to distinguish the Gospel from the Law, let him give thanks to God and know that he is a theologian. Indeed, in temptation, I do not yet know it as I should. Similar [is the ability to] carefully distinguish the righteousness of the Gospel from the righteousness of the Law, which God has as carefully separated as heaven from earth, light from darkness, day from night; and would that we could still further distinguish them." This is LUTHER. And what other light has dispelled the densest darkness of the Papal kingdom, if not chiefly this, that the true difference between the Law and the Gospel has been demonstrated?

However, we will set aside those matters that Paul addresses about the comparison of the Old and New Testament in 2 Corinthians 3:13 and following and in Hebrews concerning things such as promulgation, time, and place because they do not directly relate here, and we will enumerate the principal distinct points by which the doctrine of the Gospel is to be distinguished from the Law:

1. The doctrine of the Law is in some way naturally known to reason, but the Gospel is a mystery hidden for ages and now revealed through the ministry of the Spirit.

2. LUTHER rightly and eloquently states that both doctrines deal with sin, but in different ways. For the Law shows, accuses, imputes and condemns sin. The Gospel, however, forgives, covers and does not impute sin because it shows the Lamb of God who takes away the sins of the world.

3. Paul in Romans 3:27, 4:4, and 10:5 shows this distinction. The doctrine of the Law is the law of works, which preaches about doing: "The person who does these things will live by them," and it imputes the reward of doing. But the Gospel is the law of faith because, to the one who does not work but believes in Him who justifies the ungodly, faith is credited as righteousness.

4. The Law prescribes and demands from each individual perfect obedience to all the commandments of God, and threatens with a curse those who do not have such conformity with the will of God. However, because the Law is weakened by the flesh, the Gospel shows Christ, who is made sin and a curse under the Law and is the fulfillment of the Law for righteousness to everyone who believes.

5. The promises of the Law are conditional, but the Gospel's promise of forgiveness of sins is free.

6. The Law concludes under sin, makes the whole world guilty before God, works wrath, subjects to a curse, and is the administration of death and damnation. The Gospel, however, is the word of salvation, peace, and reconciliation liberates from the law of sin and death; and is the administration of righteousness and the Spirit.

7. The Law shows what good works are, in which God wishes the reborn to exercise obedience. The Gospel, however, teaches how they can be accomplished, for it contains the promise of the Spirit of renewal, who writes the Law in the hearts of believers. It also teaches how the obedience now begun, although it is imperfect and in many ways tainted, is pleasing to God in those who are justified by faith for the sake of Christ.

8. The Law preaches to hypocrites, the complacent, and the old man, but the Gospel preaches to the poor in spirit, the contrite, the broken, and the captives and retains the new man under grace.

I consider these to be the main points of difference. And now the true foundations of this question, namely, what the proper doctrine of the Gospel is that must be distinguished from the Law, are clear. Paul says that the righteousness of God is revealed in the Gospel apart from the Law; therefore, although in the teachings of Christ and the Apostles many sermons about the recognition of sin and about good works are found, these are not the proper doctrine of the Gospel, as far as it is distinguished from the Law. Why the commandments of the Law are found in the preaching of the Gospel, we will say later.

However, by thus separating those things that properly pertain to the ministry of the Law, distinguishing it [i.e., the Gospel] from the Law becomes easy and straightforward, insofar as it preaches about the benefits of Christ and reveals the righteousness of faith before God. And thus the Apology states clearly, "The Gospel, which is properly the promise of the forgiveness of sins and justification for the sake of Christ, preaches the righteousness of faith in Christ."[*]

However, we will divide these points into certain sections, so that the explanation may be simpler and clearer:

---

[*] Apology IV:43.

1. The Gospel preaches to the penitent regarding the free promise of reconciliation, forgiveness of sins, righteousness before God, salvation, and acceptance to eternal life, which promise is founded on the grace, mercy, and love of God (Ephesians 1:6 and 2:8; Titus 3:5; 2 Timothy 1:9).

2. In the definition of the Gospel, the Person of Christ must always be included, particularly in the role of Mediator, for in Him all promises are "Yes" and "Amen." (2 Corinthians 1:20). The New Testament is confirmed in Christ (Galatians 3:17). And here, those benefits of Christ for which we receive forgiveness of sins and are accepted for eternal life must necessarily be distinguished from the benefits of sanctification, or renewal, which follow justification. For we are not justified by these; that is, we do not receive forgiveness of sins, nor are we accepted for eternal life because of the subsequent renewal, although it is also a benefit of Christ. But the benefits of reconciliation are, first, that Christ transfers our sins and the punishment of our sins onto Himself and satisfies the Father for them, and second, that it is the fulfillment of the Law for righteousness to everyone who believes. For by these benefits of Christ, believers are reconciled to God and accepted for eternal life.

3. The Gospel teaches that these benefits of the Mediator are to be grasped by faith and applied to those who repent.

4. The Gospel teaches that these benefits are offered through the Word and Sacraments, by which instruments the Holy Spirit is effective, enlightens hearts, works faith, persuades hearts with life-giving consolation, uplifts, and sustains.

5. After the benefit of grace or Justification, the Gospel also contains the promise of the gift by grace (Rom. 5:17), or of truth (John 1:17), namely, that the Spirit of renewal, who writes the Law in their hearts, is poured out on believers so that we might be His

workmanship, created in Christ Jesus for good works, which God prepared beforehand that we should walk in them.

6. The Gospel not only preaches about the present benefits that we receive by faith for the sake of Christ in this life, but also holds the promise of the hope of righteousness that we await (Gal. 5:5), [in which] God will be all in all (1 Cor. 15:28), and of the hope of the glory of God, which will be revealed to us in the future life (Rom. 5:2 and 8:18).

7. The promise of the Gospel is universal, pertaining to all, both Gentiles and Jews, who repent and receive the promise by faith.

Because these foundations of the doctrine of the Gospel are true, so also it is necessary for them to be diligently retained in the Church. Otherwise, the purity of the doctrine of Justification cannot be preserved, because once a delusion is admitted in this matter, the corruption of the article on Justification immediately follows, as we showed briefly at the beginning.

VII.
On the Common Definition, That the Gospel is the Preaching of Repentance and the Forgiveness of Sins.*

This way of speaking is repeated several times in the Augsburg Confession and its Apology, and it cannot nor should be simply rejected and condemned, so that no true and suitable explanation is admitted. For when commending the teaching ministry to the Apostles after the resurrection in Matthew 28:20, Christ mentions Teaching and Baptism, and adds, "Teaching them to observe all that I have commanded you." He also names the sum of this ministry [to be] the Gospel, in Mark 16:16, where He explicitly adds, "Whoever does not believe will be condemned." And He says in Luke 24:47 that repentance and forgiveness of sins should be preached in His name.

However, here it must be considered what we have said above, how the Papists and others lay traps with such general descriptions, so that we should tread carefully and wisely. For Islebius**, from that definition understood in a perverse way, tried to construct his Antinomianism, as his theses show. And there indeed, LUTHER would have had the opportunity to reject and condemn this common definition in general and outright if he had judged it to be a corruption of the true and sound doctrine. However, because he preferred to explain it with a true and suitable declaration, and to refute the perverse understanding or misuse, it is evident what must be done rightly and piously in this controversy, following the example of LUTHER.

---

* As with the preceding chapter, this chapter relates to FC Epitome and Solid Declaration V, and also Article VI, "Of the Third Use of the Law."
** Johannes Agricola (A.D. 1494–1566), sometimes referred to as "Magister Islebius" after his birthplace, Eisleben. The father of the Antinomian heresy, Agricola set the pattern for many heretics to follow: give the appearance of attacking Philipp Melanchthon, when the true target is Luther's teaching.

Therefore, they err and do not act correctly, who defend this common definition in such a way that they obscure and bury that necessary distinction of what the proper doctrine of the Gospel is. Also, those [err] who say that the Law indeed is the preaching of contrition, but a deadly and despairing kind, such as was Judas's, for the preaching of salvific contrition should be taught and learned not from the ministry of the Law, but of the Gospel. And those who argue that the Gospel, properly so called, contains not only the promise of grace but also the doctrine of good works do not understand what they are saying. In this way, the distinction between the Law and the Gospel is confused (a distinction which Paul establishes in Rom. 3:27), [and they become] the law of faith and the law of works, and the Gospel is transformed into the Law. And with these foundations upheaved, the purity of the doctrine of Justification cannot stand. And Philip [Melanchthon] himself, the author of this definition, carefully warns, "Although in the doctrine of the Gospel, of Christ and the Apostles, there are many sermons about repentance and the Law, yet another question is what is the proper doctrine of the Gospel, and [how it is] to be separated from the Law."

Therefore, we will note some points on how this common definition, which has been repeated so many times in the Augsburg Confession and its Apology, can be correctly and suitably understood and explained, so that the core principle remains uncorrupted and intact, concerning the necessary distinction between the Law and the Gospel, namely what the proper doctrine of the Gospel is, which must be distinguished from the Law, and which preaches about the benefits of the Son of God, and which reveals the righteousness of faith before God. For this must be the standard of explanation:

1. The Gospel is sometimes generally understood as the summary of the entire doctrine that was delivered and propagated through the ministry of Christ and the Apostles. And in this way,

without a doubt, this common definition is true. For in Acts 20:24, Paul says his ministry is to testify to the Gospel of the grace of God. And he lists its main points: testimony of repentance and faith in Jesus Christ. Also, in chapter 1, the Evangelist Mark calls the preaching of repentance for the forgiveness of sins the beginning of the Gospel. And when Christ taught repentance and forgiveness of sins, the Evangelists say He preached the Gospel of the kingdom of God. And yet the proper doctrine of the Gospel remains distinct from the Law. Mark 1:15: "Repent and believe in the Gospel." It is a synecdoche when the name is taken from the more important part and attributed to the entire ministry. So also LUTHER speaks in the third disputation, proposition 34, against the Antinomians: "Christ throughout the Gospel reproves, rebukes, threatens, frightens, and performs similar functions of the Law." And in the preface to the letter to the Romans, chapter 16, "God's wrath is revealed through the Gospel." Because the Gospel announces grace not to the complacent and hypocrites, but to the penitent; that is, to those who, through the recognition of sin and the feeling of God's wrath, are humbled and contrite, in this sense, it is not improperly said that the Gospel is the preaching of repentance.

And there is no doubt that this wording was repeated so many times in the Augsburg Confession with the intention to of countering the cries of the Papists, who were proclaiming that the doctrine of the Gospel nurtures carnal security and confirms the license to sin in the minds of people. Therefore, it was stated that the free forgiveness of sins requires repentance, that is, a contrite and humbled heart. And yet, Paul's assertion remains firm: "Through the Law comes the knowledge of sin," from whence the recognition of sins and contrition should be taught and learned, namely, from the ministry of the Law is another matter. So LUTHER often responds to objections in the Antinomian disputations: "The Gospel preaches repentance through the ministry of the Law." Philip

[Melanchthon] says the same in the penultimate disputation. And in the same way, it is stated in the Smalcald Articles, "The New Testament retains the ministry of the Law that accuses sins and presses it."* The Confession of Württemberg** speaks thus: "The explanation of the Law is repeated in the preaching of the Gospel of Christ, so that, with the severity of the divine Law and the corruption of nature shown, they may be stirred to seek Christ revealed in the Gospel." These certainly have no inconvenience.

2. By contrast, the Gospel reveals, by the very fact that it says no other name has been given to mankind by which they can be saved except the name of Jesus Christ, that all are enclosed under sin. And to "justify"—a judicial word—presupposes the conscience condemned and terrified by the fear of God's judgment. Thus LUTHER says, "When God says, In your seed shall all the nations be blessed, He shows that all nations are condemned in themselves. From whence, how, and why they are condemned is learned from the Law." So he expressly speaks in disputation 4 against the Antinomians, proposition 24. [He continues,] "Paul, by the very fact that he teaches all men are to be justified in Christ, argues that all men are sinners, which is the function of the Law."

3. It is certain and clear that the Gospel delivers and shows some explications of the Law, which we cannot easily and clearly gather from Moses alone. And because the Law is the doctrine of repentance, in this sense the Gospel is not inappropriately called the preaching of repentance, but in such a way that the proper doctrine of the Gospel, the promise of grace, remains. Thus LUTHER says in Galatians 2, "But the commandments found in the Gospel, these are not the Gospel, but expositions of the Law, and appendices to the Gospel."

---

* SA III, III.
** Written by Johannes Brentz (A.D. 1499–1570) for Duke Christopher in 1551. The *Württemberg Confession* had 35 articles, and was approved in Wittenberg as consistent with Melanchthon's *Saxon Confession* of the same year.

However, the explications that the Gospel adds to the Law must be observed; thus, the usual definition [of the Law] can be delivered and declared usefully and fruitfully. Regarding the use of the Law, LUTHER writes concerning Galatians 3, "The office and use of the Law is not only to show sin and the wrath of God but also to compel towards Christ. This use of the Law is sought by the Holy Spirit alone, and the Gospel shows it because only the Gospel says that God is present to a broken heart." So far LUTHER. Also, the Law prescribes and demands perfect obedience to all the commandments of God. This is done to this end: not that we presume on our own strengths, as if we could fulfill it, but to exclude all boasting, and to learn that we cannot be justified by our works, and therefore we need another righteousness before God. Indeed, we cannot take this [understanding] from the Law alone unless it is illuminated by the doctrine of the Gospel. Because the Law prescribes and demands such obedience, and does not expressly say that it is impossible for us, but adds the promises of life to those who fulfill it, the hypocritical mind, if it has only the Law, judges that it can provide that obedience because God does not mock us by commanding and promising in the Law, as Erasmus says, and as the Pharisee feels in Luke 18:16. And this is the veil that Paul says is placed over the reading of the Old Testament, unless it is revealed and removed in Christ (2 Corinthians 3:13 and following). Romans 3:27 says in clear words that boasting is excluded by the law of faith. So LUTHER says in Galatians 4, "The Law says: 'The one who does these things will live by them.' But the Gospel says, 'You do not do these things. Therefore, you will not live by it.'" When we have learned this from the declaration of the Gospel, then we can also see the foundations in the Law itself, how the perfect fulfillment of the Law is impossible for us.

And there is also this one explanation that the law of faith adds to the law of works, namely, that not only those vices which directly oppose the Law of God but also external respectable conduct in the unregenerate are sin, according to these statements: "Without faith it is impossible to please God," and, "Whatever is not from faith is sin." And as John 16:8–9 states, the Holy Spirit will convict the world of sin even in the most honorable life, because it [the world] does not believe in Christ. These are indeed legal matters, but without the explanation of the Gospel (which is the doctrine of faith), they would not be understood in the Law.

Moreover, it is certain and noteworthy that only the doctrine of faith shows the distinction between mortal and venial sin. For the Law, as Law, although consent does not accompany but resists, speaks thus even regarding the smallest deeds: "Whoever keeps the whole Law but fails in one point has become guilty of all of it." Also: "Cursed be anyone who does not confirm the words of this Law by doing them." And the source of error among the Scholastics is that they established the distinction between mortal and venial sin without regard to faith, from the Law alone.

4. Also, to the Law's doctrine of good works, the Gospel adds this clarification; namely, how they can be accomplished. For concerning the Law, Moses says in Deuteronomy 29:2–4, "You have seen and heard, but God has not given you a heart to understand or eyes to see." But about the New Testament, the Prophet says, "I will write my law in their hearts" (Jeremiah 31:33). However, how the obedience begun in believers, although it is imperfect and in many ways defiled, is pleasing to God, is certainly not a legal doctrine, for the Law teaches that obedience is pleasing to God only when it is performed with such perfection from the whole heart, and without any concupiscence, as the Law dictates, and that otherwise, it is considered a transgression against the Law.

Moreover, the promises of the Law concerning the rewards for good works, because they demand the condition that nothing contrary to the Law be committed at all, would become void for us unless we learned from the Gospel how we are deemed righteous and how initial obedience according to the Law is pleasing to God. Thus, individuals are justified by faith, on account of Christ, and the promises of the Law are confirmed because God accepts their obedience. These points can indeed be usefully and fruitfully addressed in the explanation of the common definition [of the Gospel]. Nevertheless, the essential distinction between these appendices of the Gospel (as LUTHER calls them) and the proper doctrine of the Gospel, which reveals the righteousness of faith before God, must remain preserved and intact.

5. The Law, in the first table, broadly condemns all disbelief in the Word of God. The Gospel, however, when creating a contrast with the doctrine of faith, specifically points out that disbelief, which rejects the free promise of reconciliation and does not believe in the Son of God, is the supreme and greatest sin, which also causes all other sins not to be forgiven and makes even the most honorable life a sin before God. Many such contrasts are found in the Gospel: "Whoever does not believe in the Son, the wrath of God remains on him." Also, "Whoever does not believe will be condemned." Also, "This is the judgment, that light has come into the world, and people loved the darkness rather than the light." It is certain, however, that the Law, as Law, does not preach the free promise of reconciliation or the benefits of Christ the Mediator. Therefore, these are antitheses of the Gospel doctrine, not of the Law. For affirmative trust in free mercy for the sake of Christ is not the voice of the Law, as Paul clearly says in Gal. 3:12, "The Law is not of faith." For that trust, which the first commandment, as the Law of Laws, teaches in a proper sense, is not that Gospel proclamation: "Take heart, son; your sins are forgiven." But it indeed establishes that God is good and merciful to those who provide the Law with perpetual and perfect obedience. But also the work of faith in Christ and the sin of the opposite disbelief are related to

the first commandment. LUTHER [write in his commentary on] in Genesis 22, fol. 303, "Because the Law generally preaches that one should believe in the Word of God, and not to believe is a sin." Thus, what LUTHER says stands: "Whatever shows sin, wrath, or death performs the function of the Law, whether it be in the Old or New Testament." In this manner, not believing in Christ is a sin against the first commandment, for the declaration of that disbelief is shown by the antitheses of the Gospel. Also, because the Gospel imputatively grants to believers in Christ that perfect obedience which the Law requires, faith is related to the first commandment. These points are true and straightforward without sophistry. But if someone is fond of arguing, they can evade not just these points but even those that are clearer.

6. LUTHER in the first disputation against the Antinomians, shows through several theses in what sense and for what reasons it is rightly said, "The Gospel is the preaching of repentance"; namely, that contrition should be salutary and repentance for salvation must include the voice of the Gospel. I will note several theses: "1. Repentance, by all testimony and truly, is sorrow for sin, with the addition of a purpose for a better life. ... 7. The first part of repentance, namely sorrow, comes only from the Law; the second part, namely good purpose, cannot come from the Law. 8. Repentance solely from the Law is half or the beginning of repentance, or by synecdoche repentance, because it lacks a good purpose. 9. And if it persists, it is the repentance of Cain, Saul, Judas, and all who despair. ... 21. Therefore, against the useless and despairing teachers, the Gospel began to teach that repentance should not be merely despair. 22. But the penitent should conceive hope, and thus hate sin out of love for God. This is truly a good purpose. 23. Some, not considering the empty way of speaking, or the subject matter, thought this was spoken against the Law."

I consider this to be a simple, true, useful, and beneficial resolution of this controversy regarding the definition of the Gospel.

VIII.
On the Article of Justification.*

The main controversy in this article is about Osiandrianism. And indeed, the corruptions of Andreas Osiander (otherwise an exceptional man) in this article on Justification are so gross, notorious, and forceful that even the less learned, who at least have learned the catechism of sound doctrine, can notice them; hence, they have also been censured and condemned by almost all church councils, for the author of these corruptions openly professed to disagree with the Augsburg Confession in the doctrine of Justification. We do not unravel what has been rightly condemned, as if we seek endless disputes, but because various writings are scattered not only almost every year, but nearly every month, both in Latin and German, in which the harmful corruptions of Osiander are painted with artful colors and presented in a new guise, to allies and adversaries alike, indeed even to the uneducated populace through German pamphlets; therefore, it is absolutely necessary, in accordance with the healthy advice of the Church, to establish one true and certain opinion, which is useful for retaining and propagating the truth of the sound doctrine of Justification, against all nurseries of corruption, regarding what should be thought about this controversy according to the standard of God's Word. For what, I ask, are we building, when we paint over things we cannot defend with borrowed colors, as Ezekiel speaks of the plastering of a crumbling wall, so that faults do not appear to the buyer, just as the hired rhetoricians of old sought a display of wit in ἀδόξοις (undistinguished) matters.

---

* This chapter addresses the Osiandrian Controversy, which is the primary topic of FC Epitome and Solid Declaration Article III, "Of the Righteousness of Faith Before God."

If Osiander's opinion on Justification by faith, which he set against the Augsburg Confession, is true, let it be clearly demonstrated. But if it does not align with the prophetic and apostolic teaching, why do we seek [it] with so much trouble to the Church, when we have wise remedies in the same words [of Scripture] for the one who is sick? For that craft, which the Prophet calls "plastering," is neither beneficial nor healthy for the Church. For by this means, many are further entrenched in false opinions previously held and the audacity to undermine truths and to fabricate absurdities is incited and fed. Some also begin to doubt the entire body of doctrine when they see that in the chief articles of our faith, it is treated the same whether one affirms or denies. In this manner, even our Papal adversaries reproach us with this inconsistency—and not entirely without basis. But if anyone believes that by this means the purity of doctrine can be maintained and passed on to future generations, they are seriously mistaken. For Christ demands of us both to hear the true voice and to flee from the stranger's voice. And Paul requires in a teacher of the Church, not only to hold fast to sound doctrine, but also to be able to reprove—ἐλέγχθν (to refute)—those who contradict. Indeed, when 2 Timothy 1:13 prohibits τό ἑτεροδιδασκαλειν (to teach differently), he is speaking not only of false opinions, but also of the form of teaching handed down by the Apostles, which should not be carelessly altered or recklessly disrupted.

However, it is worthwhile to consider by what arguments they attempt to advocate for the Osiandrian cause, in order to prove that Osiander's opinion on the righteousness of faith has been unjustly condemned by so many Churches. And a refutation is necessary for the sake of warning, even for future generations, so that it is not judged to be a trivial contest and a harmless play of wits to teach differently (ἑτεροδιδασκαλειν) in the article of Justification. For the fate of a declining Church threatens many such things, which certainly should not be confirmed by public votes.

Thus, in summary, they contend as follows: It is certain that the essence of the Gospel doctrine is that there are two kinds of benefits from Christ, namely grace and truth (John 1:17); grace, and the gift by grace (Romans 5:17), or the benefit of reconciliation, and the benefit of renewal or sanctification. They say that Osiander never denied these benefits of Christ, which are the very substance and material (so to speak) of the Gospel, but that he professed both: that in the Gospel, by faith for the sake of Christ, we receive forgiveness of sins and the Spirit of renewal. However, the only difference is that what the Augsburg Confession, following the ὑποτύπωσιν (pattern) of the apostolic phraseology, calls renewal, Osiander called justification and the righteousness of faith. And those Scriptural testimonies in the Augsburg Confession, which are correctly referred to the benefit of Christ, Osiander applied with irrelevant citation to renewal. Just as for all writers, both ancient and recent, many misapplications of testimonies must be excused, when they think correctly about the matters themselves: so Osiander's opinion, because of some improper expressions and irrelevant citations, should not rightly be condemned, when there is agreement in the matters themselves, since indeed many awkwardly and improperly stated things are tolerated in the writings of all the fathers. This is more or less the essence of the Apology which they make for Osiander.

And these things flatter at first glance, because nature is more inclined toward defense than in admitting error. But if they are considered more closely, not only will they seem to be fig leaves sewn together, but it will also be clear that these were concocted for any and all crafty corruptions of the article on the righteousness of faith. For I find exactly the same in the writings of Gropper, who affirms that he believes and confesses that we receive both reconciliation and renewal through faith on account of Christ alone, for these are the benefits of Christ alone. But his contention is only this: Testimonies about Justification, or the righteousness of faith, encompass both the forgiveness of sins and renewal because the Gospel preaches about the whole benefit of Christ, about grace and the gift through grace. And it is evident that if we permit that defense which we mentioned for Osiander, we could in no way rightfully object to Gropper. Yet, this is a manifest perversion of the doctrine of the righteousness of faith. And I mention this example so that in it the danger and inconvenience of such seeming artful reconciliations may be considered.

Nor should it be considered an empty λογομαχία [logomachy] when, in the article of Justification, words are twisted from their true, genuine, and apostolic meaning into a foreign sense. For there should be a perpetual admonition to the Church of all times, that when Augustine, who yet had some light beyond others, slightly deviated from the native and apostolic meaning of the words "justification" and "righteousness," there followed those sad and dreadful darknesses in the Papal realm about the righteousness of faith. And LUTHER admits that he sweated much and long in the gravest trials to establish from Scripture that the righteousness of faith signifies not a substance or quality in us, but a relation. And in sum, by this means, God again kindled the light of the Gospel, whereby the words "justification," "righteousness," "grace," and "faith" were restored to their true and apostolic sense. How easily, then, will we again lose that light if we sanction by public decrees that those words in the principal testimonies can, without endangering faith, be taken and explained in this or that way, or in any manner whatsoever? For without grammar, the necessary matters in the article of Justification cannot be retained in true purity.

Moreover, there is a great difference between catachreses*, which are admitted without detriment to the true meaning, and cases in which, along with the words, the very matters themselves

---

* Plural of catachresis, meaning the use of the wrong word for the context.

are moved from the place which Scripture assigns to them and are transferred elsewhere, especially in those testimonies in which there is the principal seat and foundation of an article of faith, as in the testimonies concerning the righteousness of faith. Thus Pelagius was justly condemned when he departed from the meaning of the words of Romans 5, although he constructed a not in itself impious doctrine about the contagions of vices, because that passage is the seat [sedes] of the doctrine of Original Sin. And just as the matters themselves are revealed through the words, so without the true and apostolic meaning of the words, they cannot be understood or retained, especially in those places where the articles of faith are founded, as in their proper seat. And such beyond all controversy are those places (e.g., Genesis 15:6; Romans 3:22, 24, and 25; Romans 4:3; Romans 5:1; John 16:8; Philippians 3:9) which Osiander distorted with his interpretation. These certainties are so evident that they cannot be evaded by any sophistry.

And yet, even if this [i.e. catachresis] were the cause, Osiander's deed should not be defended as a praiseworthy act in public monuments. However, Osiander himself does not even accept that minimal mitigation of his supporters, and it is useful for the state of the Osiandrian dispute to be known from his own writings to all posterity. Therefore, Osiander himself, in his confession and refutation against Philip [Melanchthon], expressly states that the status or κρινόμενον [the matter judged] of his dispute is not that we receive by faith the forgiveness of sins and acceptance to eternal life on account of Christ's obedience; nor is the state of the controversy about the renewal, which is through the indwelling of the divinity, for he admits that doctrine is correctly taught by our side; nor is the question about righteousness in the future life. (These [admissions] are found in Osiander's refutation against Philip, fol. E. 2. L. 2. M. 2., 3. N. 2. P. 2., and 3. S. 3.) But he says this is the state of his dispute: What that righteousness of God or of faith is, which is revealed in the Gospel and which is founded on the testimonies of Gen. 15; Rom. 3, 4, [and] 5; Phi. 3; and John 16. He contends not only about words but attributes to this righteousness, of which he disputes, those very characteristics that Paul does; namely, that by it we are justified before God for eternal life, and that righteousness delivers from death, which righteousness follows, and life and eternal salvation must necessarily follow. (These are from Osiander's *confession*,* fol. G. 1. H. 3. O. 3. S. 4. T. 2. 3. 4. V. 2. 4. In the *refutation***, D. 4. G. 3. H. 1. M. 2.)***

Thus, the controversy was not about the question of *whether* there is forgiveness of sins and renewal through the benefit of Christ. But it was about the question of *what* it is; namely, what that thing is for which we are justified before God for eternal life, and freed from death: Whether it is the imputation of Christ's obedience or, indeed, the renewal through the Holy Spirit. So, the dispute is about a very great matter. For there is no greater treasure, neither in heaven nor on earth, than that the doctrine has been revealed to us, miserable sinners, concerning how we are justified freely before God by faith for eternal life.

Here Osiander scornfully lashes out at, disapproves of, rejects, and condemns the doctrine of the Augsburg Confession because it asserts that the righteousness of faith before God is the imputation of Christ's obedience. He calls this doctrine of the Augsburg Confession "carnal," "physical," "phantasmal," "idolatrous," "teaching a painted and fictitious Christ in the kingdom of the devil," and adds many more atrocious things to these. These are found

---

* Osiander's *Von dem einigen Mittler Jesu Christo* (1551).

** Osiander's *Widerlegung Der ungegrundten undienstlichen Antwort Philippi Melanchtonis* (1552).

*** Chemnitz's various citation references use the old system of 'folios' and 'signatures' for page references, which was the system used by publishers before the use of page numbers.

in very many places in Osiander's writings, in the *Confession* (fol. G. 1. 2. I. last); in the *Refutation* (K. 1. O. 4); and *Schmeckbier** (H.2). He himself asserts that the righteousness of faith, which delivers from death, by which Paul says the ungodly is justified before God for eternal life (For Osiander also attributes these to his own righteousness, about which he disputes), is an infused righteousness, in which all virtues are included, which makes us do just acts and mortifies sins, and this righteousness is the divine essence, dwelling in believers, and indeed it brings it about that we act justly. That this is Osiander's opinion, not even his patrons can deny.

And indeed, it is lamentable that the fate of this age is so deplorable that it calls into question and debate whether such corruptions, which so explicitly and atrociously attack, undermine, and pervert the principal article of our doctrine, should be censured and condemned. For if it is to be said in the gentlest terms, it is sophistry to gloss over such notorious, such dreadful corruptions with the misuse of irrelevant testimonies, as if it were just like those who think correctly, whether through negligence or while engaged in other matters, often let slip statements that are awkward and improper.

If this method of reconciliation becomes accepted and customary in ecclesiastical disputes, then Postellus, who wrote *De orbis terrae concordia***, in which he reconciles all the religions of all nations as if they were true and genuinely in agreement, and by this means promises world harmony (as he titles his book) will

---

* *Schmeckbier* was a 1552 work of Osiander in which he attacked Joachim Mörlin (Chemnitz's Superintendent in 1561) and other faithful Lutherans because of their critique of his novel teachings regarding Justification. Mörlin had attempted to stay out of the Osiandrian controversy because of Osiander's prior faithfulness; however, he felt compelled to take a public stand in 1552, and Osiander attacked him.

** Guillaume Postel (1510–1581), a French Kabbalist and Universalist who was affiliated with the early Jesuits (though he did not ultimately enter their order), wrote this work in 1544.

be the best artist of reconciliation. But what will future generations learn from these examples, if there are to be any? Therefore, I would not want to wound my conscience either by approval or by excusing such distortions, which are known to conflict with true doctrine and provide a breeding ground for many errors in that article which is the true base and foundation of our entire religion. And thus we conclude regarding Osiandrianism.

Furthermore, eloquent phrases that either obscure or corrupt the purity of the article on Justification, which have been introduced in any way into the crystal-clear fountains of the Augsburg Confession from the reservoirs of the Papacy through rivals of impious interfaith [*impiae interreligionis*], must be categorically rejected, both because of current conflicts and for the warning of future generations, like this notion of Gropper referenced in some of our writings: That the justification by faith, by which we are reconciled to God and accepted for eternal life, consists and is completed by these two parts, reconciliation and renewal, from which good works, that is, the fruits of the Spirit, ensue. For this is a clear corruption of the righteousness of faith.

For although renewal ought to follow, and undoubtedly does follow, it is certain from the Word of God that individuals are not reconciled before God or accepted for eternal life because of the subsequent renewal, but by faith alone they grasp the free promise of forgiveness of sins, through and because of Christ. And this tenet must be rejected: That the application of the free promise occurs simultaneously with the faith of the heart and the confession of the mouth. For this is nothing else but to say that the promise of grace is not apprehended and applied by faith alone.

That statement which somehow slipped out (that the Papists are rebuked because they teach as if a man is not primarily justified and accepted before God by faith on account of his own virtues) because it is awkwardly and ambiguously phrased no matter how it is softened, should not be defended as a ὑποτύπωσις [pattern] of sound words. But this opinion, which is found in a certain disputation of Philip [Melanchthon] regarding the antithesis of human opinions and the true understanding regarding Justification. Where this opinion is expressly rejected and condemned— the one that teaches people are principally righteous by faith, that is, by trust in mercy, and less principally, on account of the dignity of works; because no one satisfies the Law, and therefore the trust in mercy compensates for what is lacking—should be repeated and retained.* This is stated there.

It is also questioned whether it has been rightly said that one should not fight over the word "Alone [*Sola*]." And it is true, in a certain disputation about faith overcoming doubt, held many years ago during the time of LUTHER, these words exist about the word "Alone": "We do not quarrel so much about words, but we wish to retain them so that good minds understand they have no condemnation and are pleasing to God on account of the Son, by His faith, not on account of the Law, or because of virtue, worthiness." And in this way, it is correctly said that the dispute over this proposition—that is, that we are justified by faith alone—is not a λογομαχίαν [logomachy] but concerns a very grave matter and is of utmost necessity for the conscience. However, during the Interim period when the doctrine of Justification was attacked with various tricks, the word "Alone" was to be either concealed or omitted, and other ways of speaking were to be used instead, as cannot be denied, there was then a profound silence of this proposition, and the word "Alone" was hardly ever faintly heard. In this manner and with this understanding, that statement is not rightly defended.**

---

* In other words, Melanchthon's *condemnation* of the expressed Papist notion (that people are principally righteous by faith, that is, by trust in mercy, and less principally, on account of the dignity of works) should be retained.

** The point is that while at an earlier period, Luther rightly declared "we do

For there are true and necessary reasons why the exclusion "By faith alone" must be retained, namely: 1. to give due honor to the Son of God, that His sacrifice alone is the price for us; 2. that consciences may have firm consolation; 3. that the distinction between the Law and the Gospel may be seen; 4. that invocation may be made, which is hindered by the sight of our weakness. And since in the conflict against the Papists these issues are mainly and primarily discussed, the word "Alone" should not be ignored or discarded in such matters.

Furthermore, there is debate over the following proposition: "That faith, which possesses connected love, hope, and the other virtues, justifies." However, it is evident that there is a very dangerous ambiguity in this proposition. For with these formulas, the Papists now depict *formed* faith, and thus they speak when they want it to be understood—not faith *alone*, but faith *with the other virtues*, justifies. And this pious and religious caution should be noted for posterity. When at the Colloquy of Regensburg a book proposed thus spoke—"The sinner is justified by living and effective faith"—our side, by the counsel and warning of LUTHER, did not want to accept that proposition due to its twisting ambiguity because it could easily be perverted to mean, "effective faith or working faith, that is, faith with works, justifies a man."

However, it must also be considered that such an antithesis to this proposition should not be presented and proven, such as, "Faith, which is without works, or which does not produce good works, or which is not effective through love, justifies." For this would essentially mean, "Dead or hypocritical faith justifies."

---

not quarrel so much about words," during the Interim, when Emperor Charles V attempted to extirpate the Lutheran Reformation by means of his "Interim" which would steadily eliminate all traces of the Reformation doctrine and practice, compromising the use of that one word—Alone/*Sola*—was an indefensible betrayal of the faithful confession.

And the Apology [of the Augsburg Confession] correctly states, "Faith, which is without works, does not justify." LUTHER in his commentary on Galatians 3 says, "Because it is necessary to distinguish between true and theological faith and false or feigned faith: Nothing would trouble me if one were to distinguish formed faith against false or feigned faith; but since they understand it to mean that faith does not justify unless form, that is, love, is added, this most deadly form and Satanic gloss must be condemned." Therefore, the ambiguity of this proposition needs to be clearly explained, lest we fall into the trap of either formed faith or dead faith.

But this also must necessarily be added: Charity is not the life of faith; rather, faith that grasps Christ is in itself not a barren condition, but a fervent motion, comforting and giving life, because it grasps Christ, who is eternal life. Then, this life of faith subsequently expresses itself and becomes effective through love and the other virtues.

This proposition is also criticized: "It is necessary for the other virtues, such as hope, patience, and similar ones, to be joined with faith, and yet trust must not rely on these, but on the Son of God." However, this proposition is not correctly criticized in this manner: As if faith alone excludes the other virtues, not just from [such virtues] being merit, cause, or part of Justification, but as if it outright excludes the very presence of all other virtues, so that they are entirely absent. For there is a clear distinction when Abraham is initially called out of Chaldean idolatry, [and] at that time he had no good works. But when, after several years, he is reborn and declared righteous in Genesis 15:6, his faith certainly is accompanied by a beautiful array of virtues, and yet it is faith alone that justifies. Paul specifically chose the example of Abraham, not when he was first called from Ur of the Chaldeans, but after he had already been obeying God through faith for several years (Hebrews 11:8 and the subsequent verses). And although Abraham then had many most excellent and beautiful good works, yet in the article, matter, question, or act of Justification, Paul says of him, τῷ μὴ ἐργαζομένῳ [to the one who does not work]. Also, Abraham believes in Him who justifies the ungodly. Also, χωρὶς ἔργων [apart from works]. For there is no regard for works—whether preceding, present, or subsequent—in the article of Justification. And this proposition is simply false: "That faith, to justify or to be justifying, necessarily requires the presence of good works," for this is to construct 'formed faith,' which does not justify without works, while Paul explicitly states the contrary. And the rule is true: "Good works do not precede justification, but are its sequel or effect [*sequelam seu effectum*]." For faith is the mother of good works, as Christ says, "Make the tree good, and then the fruits good." But Paul is justified by faith alone, not only then, when in the first conversion, caught in the very act of persecution, he truly has nothing of good works, but when he is moved by the Spirit of God, walks in good works, and (as it is said in Acts about Tabitha) is full of good works, so he can truly say, "I am aware of nothing against myself." There, in the article and activity of Justification, faith turns away from any and all regard for Paul's works and grasps only the works and merits of Christ the Mediator, and in them finds rest for righteousness and salvation. And then, also those words in Romans 4:5 are truly said about Paul: "To the one who does not work but believes in Him who justifies the ungodly, his faith is counted as righteousness without works." Thus, even when it is joined with many other virtues, faith alone still justifies without works. And the distinction must necessarily be maintained, that when faith operates before God in the matter of Justification, there it does not bring along works to the act of Justification, but justifies alone without works, "To the one who does not work but believes in Him who justifies the ungodly" (Romans 4:5).

However, there is another question, regarding what argument and testimony by which we discern whether faith is true, lest we deceive ourselves with the false impression of feigned faith. Here it is rightly said that such faith is effective which works through love (Gal. 5:6). And without works, faith is dead. But in this aspect and with this regard, faith does not justify; it only justifies insofar as it apprehends the merit of Christ alone in the promise. These points, as they can, should be declared clearly, without ambiguity and sophistry, lest brevity give rise to disputes or provide breeding grounds for distortions. Thus LUTHER does concerning Genesis 15, and his words are these: "I know the other virtues are remarkable gifts of God; I know that faith does not exist without these gifts. But the question is, what is unique to each? You hold various seeds in your hand; I do not ask which are combined with which, but what is unique to each. Here state clearly, what does faith alone do, not which virtues it is combined with. But faith alone apprehends the promise; this is the unique work of faith alone. The other virtues have other matters around which they revolve." Also, "We know that faith is never alone but brings with it love and many other gifts. Thus, faith leads a choir of beautiful virtues with it, and is never alone. But for that reason, things should not be confused, and what belongs to faith alone should not be attributed to other virtues. However, faith is the mother from which that offspring of virtues is born; without her being first present, neither love nor other virtues will be present." These are LUTHER's words. Such declarations, because they edify and are necessary, must be sought and handed down.

It is also debated, more dangerously than beneficially, about the initial movements of conversion, such as contrition, detestation of sin, sorrows, recognition of God's wrath and judgment against sin, struggle, and effort, and the other movements are not good works because they are present in the apprehension of the free promise. However, good works do not precede one being justified, but follow after one is justified, given that it is certain that all these are gifts and operations of the Holy Spirit.

Furthermore, some contend that vivification must be completely removed from the article of Justification, and for this reason they criticize Philip [Melanchthon] because in Chapter 3 to the Romans, folio 8, he included vivification in the definition of Justification with these words: "Along with acceptance, the Son of God is also effective, pronouncing consolation through the voice of the Gospel in the mind, and vivifies the believer, and pours the Holy Spirit into the heart." But in exactly the same manner and with the same words does the Apology speak, linking Justification and vivification, and this multiple times, such as on folio 16, 21, 22, 30. So too, the Confession and Apology of Magdeburg published in the year 1556 says, "by this faith alone the heart is further also vivified by eternal life, conceives new and true consolation." Also, "Faith is properly the justification of the one feeling his righteousness, consolation of the terrified, vivification of the conscience killed by the Law." And indeed, the Apology of the Augsburg Confession explicitly declares what is comprehended by the term vivification in the article on Justification, for it says, "When Habakkuk says, The righteous shall live by his faith, it means that faith justifies, and it justifies in such a way that it also vivifies, that is, it raises up, consoles consciences, and produces eternal life and joy in the soul." Likewise, "Terrified minds are raised up and vivified by faith." Also, "It overcomes the terrors of sin and eternal death, liberates from death, and begets new life in hearts. For the consolation of faith is a spiritual and new life."

Nor is the manner of expression ἄγραφος [unwritten], for Habakkuk says, "The righteous shall live by his faith." Ephesians 2:5, "Even when we were dead in our trespasses, made us alive together with Christ; by grace you have been saved." 1 Samuel 2:6, "The Lord kills and brings to life." Isaiah 57:15, "To revive the spirit of the lowly, and to revive the heart of the contrite." Psalm 71:20, "You who have made me see many troubles and calamities will revive me again." And soon adds an explanation: "You have turned and comforted me." And so it is used several times in the Psalms. From this it is evident that the definition is true.

But they say that "vivification" can be understood as "new obedience." I answer that the question is what the proper meaning is, and as we have shown from Scripture, it does not primarily signify new obedience. However, it is true that new life begets new actions, as Paul says in Romans 6:5 and 7:4, and this subsequent newness does not pertain to the definition of Justification. Therefore, a clarification must be added about what vivification, which is joined to Justification, is, and that the subsequent newness does not enter into Justification. And, in this way, there will be no danger or inconvenience.

In the same way, many argue about regeneration as if to completely separate it from Justification, understanding it only in terms of subsequent newness. But LUTHER explicitly says in the first disputation on faith: "Justification is indeed a kind of regeneration." And so the Apology also speaks: "To justify means to regenerate." And Paul, when he names Baptism "the washing of regeneration and renewal," shows that regeneration and renewal are not entirely the same. For he immediately adds: "That, being justified by His grace, we might become heirs according to the hope of eternal life." Surely, we do not achieve this because of the subsequent newness. Therefore, the Pauline phraseology is that Justification and regeneration are synonymous; so it is [also] used in 1 Peter 1:3. And it is very important to retain the proper meaning of the word "regeneration," for when Scripture says in John 1:12, "He gave the right to become children of God, to those who are born of God," [and in] John 3:5, "Unless someone has been born of water and the Spirit," etc., if regeneration in these places is taken for the subsequent newness, the article of Justification will be overturned.

Therefore, in these terms, one should not deviate from the usage of Scripture.

However, it must be added that regeneration, as LUTHER says, first encompasses adoption or acceptance. Then, as a consequence, it also includes a new creation or the following renewal. For regeneration makes a new man, or a new creature, giving a new heart. Hence, new actions or new movements follow. It is evident, though, that this new creature in us is not the thing on account of which we are justified; that is, accepted for eternal life. Therefore, to prevent any possibility of error, it is always necessary to add explanations that are consistent with Scripture, to define what we mean by the term "regeneration." For in the Church, we must not speak in cunning deception, as Paul says in Ephesians 4:14, but everything should contribute to edification.

Other customary and not inconvenient expressions in this article [of faith] are also disparaged [i.e., by Osiandrians], such as when faith is said to be our Justification. Indeed, LUTHER often speaks in this way in Galatians and in the Apology on folios 19 and 41.

This statement too is criticized: "Righteousness is to believe that Christ has died and risen for you." But Paul also speaks in this manner.

There are those who argue that only one particular expression should be used, disapproving and rejecting all others, as when it is said, "Christ is our righteousness," "the death of Christ," "the blood of Christ," while Scripture itself describes the sole righteousness of faith with various terms. Yet, these terms are rightly referred to for a clearer and more comprehensive explanation of what the righteousness of faith is.

IX.
On Good Works.*

In this matter, the principal controversy concerns the proposition: "Good works are necessary for salvation, such that no one has ever been saved without good works; and even now it is not possible for anyone to be saved without good works."

Nor indeed from insolence, the desire to disagree, the inclination to contradict, or for the sake of idle subtleties, or vain quarrels over words [λογομαχίας] were disputes about these propositions initiated, when they were imposed on our churches at the most inopportune time of persecution, at that time when the Papists both by force and deceit laid traps for the purity of the doctrine of our churches. But there are true, serious, and necessary reasons why those propositions, under whatever pretext they are presented, should not be tolerated in the Church. And it is useful to repeat and make known those reasons for the sake of reminding future generations.

1. Therefore, beyond controversy, it is true that the proper distinction between the Law and the Gospel is so necessary that, with it either removed or at least obscured and adulterated, it is impossible to retain the purity of the doctrine of Justification by faith, as the histories of all times, and especially the more-than-Egyptian darkness in the Pontifical realm, show. And in our time, the purity of sound doctrine has been restored primarily by showing the true distinction between the Law and the Gospel. The Law is the doctrine of works (Romans 3:27). Its essence is this: "The person who does these things will live by them" (Romans 10:5). To the scribe asking, "What must I do to inherit eternal life?," Christ

---
* See Formula of Concord Epitome and Solid Declaration, Article IV: "Of Good Works."

responds, "Do this which is written in the Law, and you will live." Similarly, Romans 2:13: "Doers of the Law will be justified before God." Therefore, the very doctrine of the Law is: "Good works are so necessary for salvation that without them it is impossible for anyone to be saved."

Nor does the distinction between the Law and the Gospel consist in this: That good works, which by themselves are not sufficient for salvation, receive such an addition from faith in Christ, so that when Christ does what is lacking in the righteousness of our works, then we are justified and saved by faith *with* works; or by faith, but *not without* our works. For, in this way, Christ would only be a supplement to our righteousness, something patched onto an old garment, as in Matthew 9:16 and Isaiah 64:6. However, Paul establishes the distinction in this way, Romans 4:5: "To the one who does not work but believes in Him who justifies the ungodly, his faith is credited as righteousness." Also, "Blessed is the man to whom God credits righteousness apart from works." And in Romans 3:24 and 27, he says, "God justifies him who is of the faith of Jesus, so that all boasting is excluded, not by the law of works, but by the law of faith." Similarly, in verse 28: "We conclude that a man is justified by faith apart from the deeds of the law." And the false apostles among the Galatians did not completely reject faith in Christ from the article of Justification, nor did they attribute righteousness before God and salvation to works alone, separate from faith, but, as LUTHER says concerning St. Paul's Epistle to the Galatians, they taught that in addition to faith in Christ, the works of the divine Law are also necessary for salvation, Galatians 3:3: "Having begun by the Spirit, are you now being perfected by the flesh?" And yet, Paul says of that doctrine that it renders the grace of God null and void, as if Christ had died for no purpose if righteousness before God and salvation are not attributed to faith in Christ alone. And in Galatians 5:4, he says that Christ is of no benefit to such people. From this foundation, the judgment of this proposition, which asserts that good works are so necessary for salvation that without them it is impossible for anyone to be saved, is clear. For this is the very confusion of Law and Gospel against which Paul so vehemently fights.

    2. Paul, who with truly apostolic fervor often emphasizes the necessity of good works in the justified, yet in the matter, question, cause, action, (or whatever other name it may be called) of Justification and salvation, precisely teaches, vehemently emphasizes, and defends these exclusives: "without the law," "without works," "by faith," "not from works," "freely, by grace," "not from works, but by faith" (Romans 3:20 and following; Romans 4:3, 16, etc.; Romans 5:1, 2; Galatians 5:4, 5, 6; Titus 3:5; Ephesians 2:8, 9). Therefore, these are apostolic principles: We are justified by faith, freely, without the Law, apart from works. And blessed is the man to whom God credits righteousness apart from works. And the antithesis, against which Paul so fiercely fights in the matter of justification and the business of salvation, is this very proposition: "Good works, in addition to faith [*praeter fidem*], are so necessary for salvation that it is impossible for anyone to be saved and to have blessedness without them."

    And it is sophistry in this matter to separate Justification from salvation and eternal life. "For in the Church," as Augustine elegantly says, "we must speak according to prescription." Moreover, Scripture in this article uses these words as if they were synonyms. What Christ says, "Whoever believes in me has eternal life," Paul states in Galatians 2:16 as: "We are justified by faith." Habakkuk expresses the same idea as, "The righteous shall live by his faith." The same Paul, who in Romans 3:24 says, "We are justified freely by His grace through faith," renders that idea in Ephesians 2:8 and 9 as, "By grace you have been saved through faith, not of works." 2 Timothy 1:9 says, "He saved us, not because of our works, but because of His grace." Titus 3:5 states, "He saved us, not because of righteous things we had done, but because of His mercy, that being justified by His grace," etc. Romans 4:6 declares, "Blessed is the man to whom God credits righteousness apart from works." Therefore, this is the form of the apostolic doctrine: "Just as we are justified by faith without works, so we are saved by faith without works; we are righteous, we are saved, we are blessed, by faith alone, without the Law, without works."

And it is very notable that the false apostles in Acts 15:1 presented their opinion in exactly these same words: "Unless you are circumcised and keep the Law, you cannot be saved, or be in a state of salvation." These are the firmest and most evident foundations.

Paul does not dispute over paradoxical words, but adds very weighty reasons why he removes the Law and works from the article of Justification and salvation: Romans 4:16, "so that it is by grace and the promise may be sure." Galatians 2:21, "I do not nullify the grace of God, for if righteousness were through the Law, then Christ died for no purpose." Galatians 5:4, "You are severed from Christ, you who would be justified by the Law; you have fallen away from grace."

3. Therefore, no matter how this opinion may be painted with whatever colors—whether for attaining, retaining, or preserving salvation—it conflicts with the apostolic teaching, which attributes the beginning, the maintenance, and the end of salvation to faith. Through faith we have access (Ephesians 2:8), and [as] Galatians 3:3 [states], "Having begun by the Spirit, are you now being perfected by the flesh?" [Likewise,] 1 Peter 1:5, "By the power of God we are being guarded through faith for a salvation ready to be revealed in the last time." Romans 5:2, "Through faith not only do we have access to grace, but we also stand in grace, rejoicing in hope." Galatians 2:20, "And the life I now live in the flesh

I live by faith in the Son of God." The same, "Are you so foolish? Having begun by the Spirit, are you now being perfected by the flesh?" 1 Peter 1:9, the end of faith is the "salvation of souls." Colossians 1, "In Christ you have been brought to fullness." Colossians 1:23, "If indeed you continue in the faith, stable and steadfast." For if the salvation which we have received by faith is handed over to be preserved and retained by our works, the promise will not be firm. Faith is made void, and the promise is abolished. Romans 4:16, "Therefore, it is of faith, that it might be by grace, to the end the promise might be sure to all the seed; not only to that which is of the law, but to that also which is of the faith of Abraham." So, LUTHER rightly says concerning Galatians 2, "We also concede that teaching about good works and charity is necessary, but in its own time and place: When the question is about good works outside of this fundamental article. But here the matter at hand is by what means we are justified and attain eternal life. Here we answer with Paul: By faith alone in Christ we are declared righteous, not by works of the Law or by charity, not because we reject works or charity (as our adversaries accuse us), but because in the context of this discussion we do not allow anything to shift our focus, which is what Satan seeks. Therefore, when we are now discussing the common topic of Justification, we reject and condemn works. For this topic does not at all allow for a discussion about good works. Hence, in this proposition, we simply cut off all laws and all works of the Law." These are LUTHER's words.

The same in [his commentary on] Genesis 22, folio 3, recto, where he rejects and refutes that sophism: "Although we demand works as necessary for salvation, we do not teach to trust in works." These propositions provide material and occasion either for despair or for Pharisaical boasting, which must be excluded in the matter of Justification and salvation before God. Given the hypothesis that faith indeed justifies, but for salvation good works are so necessary that without them it is impossible for anyone to be saved, the mind of the sinner in temptation will begin to debate what kind, how many, and how great works beyond faith must be possessed as necessary for the salvation they seek; and if they feel they do not have them (as in temptations the notion of works is easily shaken, so that nothing but sin, and indeed outstanding sin, appears) and yet are convinced that, beyond faith, good works are absolutely necessary for salvation, so that it is impossible to be saved without good works, what else follows, please tell me, except terrible despair? But Paul says, "Therefore, it is of faith, that the promise might be sure." For if the foundation of salvation, to any degree, however small, rests on our works, the promise will be uncertain.

And if anyone is thoroughly convinced that they possess so many and such great good works, the kind and amount that are necessary for salvation, does it not follow that there will be boasting about our works, as if without them it would be impossible for us to be saved? And thus, in the article of Justification, there will be something of ours, not solely by the grace of God. But how, then, will all boasting be excluded (Romans 3:27; 1 Corinthians 1:29)? Did not this pride send the Pharisee to hell (Luke 18:14)? These are indeed true, serious, and necessary reasons why those propositions should not be tolerated.

4. Matthew, Zacchaeus, Acolastus, the publicans, the thief on the cross, and Paul in persecution, who, when caught in their sins, are called by God's mercy and justified and saved freely by faith, certainly bring no good works to their Justification and salvation, to which they are accepted. So infants, who are reborn through water and Spirit, whom God saves (Titus 3:5)—what good works do they bring, without which it would be impossible for them to be saved? Nor, indeed, does God save them with respect to subse-

quent renewal. But the reasoning is the same because God justifies and saves all sinners who believe (Romans 3:22). Indeed, Paul says in 1 Timothy 5:10, in his conversion (in which he certainly brought no good works to righteousness and salvation), Christ showed an example to all who would believe in Him for eternal life. And in Mark 10:15, Christ says, "Whoever does not receive the kingdom of God like a child shall not enter it." Therefore, although Abraham is adorned with many good works (Genesis 15), he believes in Him who justifies the ungodly without works. And Paul, though he labored more than the others, still says, "I am not justified by this" (1 Corinthians 4:4). Therefore, these propositions are false.

5. This proposition concerning the necessity of good works for salvation should also be suspect because at all times such and precisely similar ways of speaking have sought to corrupt the healthy doctrine of Justification. And in disputes where the restoration and retention of doctrinal purity was discussed, these propositions have always been criticized and condemned. In Acts 15:1, those who were tearing down Paul's doctrine of free justification had this proposition: "Unless you observe the Law in addition to faith in Christ, you cannot be saved." This is certainly the same as, "It is impossible to be saved without good works." LUTHER states the proposition of the pseudo-apostles in Galatians in his annotations on Galatians 1 with these words: "Besides faith in Christ, works of the divine Law are necessary for salvation." Likewise, Eusebius in Book 3, Chapters 23 and 27, describes the error of Ebion. And what else is the "formed faith" of the Papists, but that faith indeed justifies and saves—but not without works?, or that faith with works, or joined with works, saves?

The Papists, having been fiercely contending for 40 years against the exclusivity of the doctrine of Justification by faith alone, have always countered with this proposition using exactly the same words: "We are not justified by faith alone; but good works are also necessary for salvation." Likewise: "Good works are necessary for salvation. Therefore, we are not justified by faith alone." All the books of the opponents are full of this. Let someone merely look at the marginal notes and indexes in their books, and they will see how the proposition of the necessity of good works for salvation has always been opposed, now for forty years, to the doctrine of free reconciliation by faith alone because of the Mediator.

The following proposition was explicitly criticized and condemned by our side: "Although trust should not be placed in merits; nevertheless, good works are necessary for salvation." The refutation exists in Menius' writing against the Anabaptists, to which Luther's preface is attached on folio 326, 1. The theologians from Münster also criticized this statement in Luther's teaching, "That faith makes one blessed without good works." But Urbanus Rhegius* answers skillfully. It [Rhegius' answer] can be found in volume 2 of Luther's works, folio 443 and subsequent pages.

It is also known for what purpose, for what reasons, and with what arguments Luther in a public disputation in the year 1536 rejected and condemned that proposition. And in the first persecution, when the Papists saw that the doctrine of Justification was so established and fortified from the Word of God that it could not be overthrown in a single assault and taken from the minds of the pious, they insidiously pressed this proposition: "Good works

---

* Urbanus Rhegius (1489–1541), was a student of Johann Eck and was an Imperial poet laureate, ordained a Catholic priest in 1520, who became a Lutheran in 1521. He was a noteworthy opponent of the Anabaptists and was present at Augsburg in 1530. He was superintendent of the Duchy of Lüneberg. His 1535 homiletical handbook has been published in an English translation: *Preaching the Reformation: The Homiletical Handbook of Urbanus Rhegius*, trans. Scott Hendrix (Milwaukee: Marquette University Press, 2003).

are necessary for salvation."* They realized that if this proposition were admitted, the ruin of the doctrine of free justification would quickly, easily, and naturally follow. And since this proposition emerged from the snares of the Pontifical interfaith intrigue** into contention, it rightly should be regarded with suspicion. These foundations show that we do not quarrel petulantly over idle logomachies against those propositions, but there are true, serious, and absolutely necessary reasons why they should not be tolerated in the Church.

And when these propositions are disapproved of and condemned, not merely condemnations should be presented, but always from these foundations, reasons must be added for why we do not wish to speak this way: "That good works are necessary for salvation."

However, it must also be explicitly added, so as not to establish such an antithesis of these propositions that either tacitly or explicitly approves [the idea] that we are justified and saved without good works and new obedience, as if a sinner, who yields to depraved desires and commits actions against conscience, even if no repentance or contrition precedes, and even if no change, whether in mind or in will, is present and follows, can still be righteous and saved, provided he believes Christ died and was resurrected. With this pious and necessary moderation, to not provide an occasion for error, either to the right or to the left, Urbanus Rhegius in his writing against the Münster theologians explained and safeguarded these propositions on both sides: "Faith alone makes blessed without good works."*** Also: "Faith cannot tolerate good works

---

* The quoted text is given in German ("*Das der glaube selig mache one gute wercke.*") emphasizing that Chemnitz is not paraphrasing their position.
** i.e., the Augsburg Interim decreed May 15, 1548.
*** "*Der Glaube machet selig one gute werck.*"

alongside it."* And the theologians from Hamburg responded thus: "If there is concern about the danger in the other opinion, which denies that good works are necessary for salvation, if care is taken to not open doors to licentiousness, misuse of freedom, and laziness in performing good works, then that view could also be omitted, and the form given by the Apostles retained, namely, 'We are justified freely, by faith, without works. By grace you have been saved, it is the gift of God.'" These are their words.

In the same way, when the proposition, "Good works are necessary to retain salvation," is rejected the true reason is as follows: You are being kept by the power of God through faith for salvation (2 Peter 1:5). But this admonition, which appears in the Augsburg Confession, must be added: "Those who yield to depraved desires and commit actions against their conscience do not retain either the Holy Spirit, or the righteousness of faith, or the confidence in mercy; and those who do not abound in the Spirit lose salvation because they lose faith and the Holy Spirit." And the *Apology* [of the Augsburg Confession] says regarding the statement from 2 Peter 1, "Peter speaks about works that follow the remission of sins, and teaches why they must be done, namely, that the calling may be secure, lest they fall from their calling if they sin again. 'Do good works,' he says, 'so that you may persevere in your calling, lest you lose the gifts of the calling which occurred earlier, not because of subsequent works, but are now retained by faith, and faith does not remain in those who lose the Holy Spirit, who fail to add repentance.'" So far the *Apology***.

And it is useful to show the true foundations for why and how those who fall into sins against conscience lose salvation, while in believers who have venial sin, there is no condemnation. Thus,

---

* "*Der Glaube mag keine gute werck bey sich vertragen.*" In other words, good works may not take credit alongside faith for Justification.

** Apology XX:90

the doctrine of the preservation and loss of salvation will be correctly and solidly understood. And LUTHER clearly declares these theological foundations: Believers do not lose salvation because of venial sins, not because venial sins by their nature do not conflict with the Law, or are not worthy of the wrath of God and eternal damnation (as the Scholastics imagine), but because, although sin dwells in their flesh, they still retain faith and repentance. They grieve over that uncleanness; they resist sinful inclinations; they seek to overcome these stains; they seek and grasp the forgiveness of sins. Since salvation and faith are preserved and retained by faith, faith is not without repentance. For this reason, the saints do not lose salvation because of venial sin because they retain the faith by which salvation is preserved. On the contrary, those who permit actions against conscience lose salvation, not because the iniquity of mortal sins exceeds God's grace, or because Christ's merit cannot remove even mortal sins, but because in mortal sins, where there is no detestation but rather delight in sin, there is no repentance, and faith does not remain in those who reject repentance, as the Apology says. True faith does not seek in Christ an excuse or pleasure for sin, but forgiveness and release from sin. Nor does the Holy Spirit dwell where there is no repentance [and thus] no faith. Thus, salvation is lost through sins against conscience because faith is lost and the Holy Spirit is expelled. Once faith is lost, the righteousness of faith cannot be retained, and grace is lost because we are kept for salvation by faith (1 Peter 1:5). "By faith we stand in grace" (Romans 5:2). And just as faith is given by the gift of the Holy Spirit through the ministry of the Word and Sacraments, so too, properly speaking, faith is nourished, grows, and is retained and preserved by the power of the Spirit through the ministry of the Word and the use of the Sacraments. However, faith also grows through the practice of good works, for, as Luther says, "Idle faith, which is not exercised, quickly dies and is extinguished."

And from this, the statement of some that "New obedience is necessary to retain faith" can rightly be judged for it is lost by sins against conscience. These are the true foundations of the doctrine of the preservation and loss of salvation received through faith, and, therefore, many intricate arguments are made about this question because these foundations are not considered carefully enough by many.

Let these axioms be true, firm, and unshaken: Just as salvation is received and preserved by faith, so it is repelled, lost, and rejected by unbelief. Just as faith is the source and mother of good works, so unbelief is the origin of evil works, and where obedience is given to the realm of sin, there faith is lost and the Holy Spirit is driven out, as is declared in the Smalcald Articles. These points can be fruitfully explained in those disputations.

This Antinomian proposition is rightly and necessarily criticized and condemned: "That new obedience in the justified is optional." Indeed, the doctrine of the Augsburg Confession must be retained and included, namely, that when we are reconciled through faith, the righteousness of good works must necessarily follow, and that initiated obedience to the Law of God is necessary in those reconciled. By the term "good works," we understand not only external actions but also internal obedience in regard to both tables of the Decalogue. And to good works belongs the mortification of the actions of the flesh, resisting vicious inclinations, and being careful not to admit anything against conscience.

Furthermore, it is not merely necessary to vociferously proclaim the necessity of good works; rather, the impious opinions associated with works must be criticized and condemned. Additionally, the true reasons must be shown from the Word of God, by the consideration of which we ourselves and others can and should be spurred to the pursuit of good works. These reasons are listed in the Apology, folio 31: "Good works should be done because God requires them; therefore, they are effects of regeneration, as Paul teaches in Ephesians 2:10. Also, good works should follow faith, as an act of thanksgiving toward God. Further, they serve to exercise faith, increase it, and make it evident to others, so that through our confession others may be encouraged to confess." LUTHER in [his commentary on] Genesis 17, page 226, says, "Works do not make a person righteous, but a righteous person performs righteous works; and yet works provide that faith is exercised in them, and through them it may increase and become robust. As Abraham performs good works, he remembers the promise of God who permits and receives us. Thus, Peter instructs [us] to make our calling sure through good works. They are evidence that grace is effective within us and that we are called and chosen. Conversely, idle faith, which is not exercised, dies and extinguishes quickly. Thus, through the works of repentance, I recognize myself as one rescued from the fire of Babel. In this manner, although this obedience does not justify, it certifies and illuminates faith so that it can be visible. Hence Revelation says: "Let him who is righteous continue to be righteous." Just as those who engage in works of unbelief become more and more unbelieving, and sin gains strength from such constant exercise, conversely, in those who practice piety, faith increases, confirming that they belong to the Church." These are the words of LUTHER.

There also exists in the booklet by Urbanus Rhegius on carefully chosen formulations of speech a listing of reasons why good works must be done by the justified.

To this recitation of reasons, testimonies should be added which lend weight to the exhortation to do good works. I will note the principal testimonies because in the recitation of reasons, different points are emphasized by others so that something certain may be established and retained according to the standard of scriptural testimonies: Romans 8:12, "We are debtors." Luke 17:10, "We have done what we ought to do." 1 Thessalonians 4:3, "This is the will of God, your sanctification." Galatians 5:22, "The fruit of the Spirit." Romans 6:22, "Having been freed from sin, you have fruit unto sanctification." Philippians 1:28, "Affliction for them is an indication of perdition, but for you of salvation, and this from God." Also, Matthew 7:16, "By their fruits you shall know them." 1 John 4:13, "By this we know that we abide in Him." John 13:35, "By this all will know that you are My disciples." Matthew 5:16, "Let your light so shine." 1 Timothy 1:19, "Some having rejected a good conscience, concerning faith have suffered shipwreck." 2 Peter 1:9–10, "For whoever lacks these things is blind and short-sighted, having forgotten the cleansing from his old sins. Therefore, brethren, be all the more diligent to make your calling and election sure." 1 Timothy 5:8, "If anyone does not provide for his own, and especially for those of his household, he has denied the faith and is worse than an unbeliever." 1 John 1:6, "If we say that we have fellowship with Him and walk in darkness, we lie." 1 John 2:4, "He who says, 'I know Him,' and does not keep His commandments, is a liar." 1 John 3:7, "Let no one deceive you, he who practices righteousness is righteous"; also v. 14, "he who does not love remains in death." Ephesians 2:10, "Created in Christ Jesus for good works." Luke 1:74, "That we, being delivered, might serve Him." Romans 8:14, "Those who are led by the Spirit of God are sons of God." Galatians 5:6, "In Christ Jesus, faith works through love." 2 Peter 1:8, "If these things are yours, etc." Ephesians 4, "You did not so learn Christ." Romans 8:13, "If you live according to the flesh, you will die." Ephesians 2:2. Colossians 3:6, "Because of these things the wrath of God comes." Also, [Galatians 5:21,] "Those who do such things will not inherit the kingdom of God." James 2:20 and 2:25, "Faith without works is dead." 1 Timothy 1:5, "Unfeigned faith [ἀνυποκρίτου]." Regarding these matters, it is necessary to give a declaration without ambiguity in these controversies. Among some, there is profound silence on this matter. Some incorrectly criticize statements, such as those who reproach that [statement], "faith is exercised and confirmed by good works." When asked about the reasons why good works should be performed, some respond, "God does not care about good works." Others say: "Good works are necessary only for this life." Also, those who play with ambiguous generality without a specific explanation say, "Good works should be done not for God, but only for the neighbor," or, "not before God, but only before the neighbor." Indeed, in the article and matter of Justification, it is rightly said, "Only faith, and not works, act with God and before God." Thus, Paul speaks in Romans 4:2, "He has glory, but not before God." However, when we speak outside this fundamental article about the good works of the justified, it is not correct to say, "Good works should not be done for God or before God, but only for the neighbor and before people," for good works are worship when they are done with the purpose of offering worship and obedience to God. This certainly is doing [something] for God. And it is a common saying that the neighbor should be loved for the sake of God. And Scripture speaks thus, [in] Matthew 10:39, "Whoever loses his life for My sake," [and in] 1 Peter 2:13, "Be subject for the Lord's sake to every human institution." And the phrase "before God [*coram Deo*]" concerning the good works of the justified is often repeated. Romans 12:17, "Respect what is right, not only before God." 1 John 3:22, "Whatever we ask we receive from Him, because we keep His commandments and do what pleases Him." Luke 1:75, "Being delivered, we might serve Him in righteousness and holiness before Him." 1 Timothy 5:4, "But if any widow has children or grandchildren, let them first learn to show godliness to their own household and to make some return to their parents, for this is pleasing in the sight of God." 2 Corinthians 4:2, "But we have renounced disgraceful, underhanded ways. We refuse to practice cunning or to tamper with God's word, but by the open statement of the truth we would commend ourselves to everyone's conscience in the sight of God." Matthew 6:1, "Beware of practicing your righteousness before other people in order to be seen by them." Therefore, true and living faith produces good works; otherwise, it is dead.

But this reminder is necessary: Works are not the life of faith, nor is faith, as if dead in itself, vivified by the addition of works. For when Paul apprehends Christ—who is Life—by faith, then Christ lives in Paul, and Paul again in Christ. Works, however, declare that faith is alive, just as heated iron, if applied to wood, burns and is found to be heated, but even if applied to no material, nonetheless it is heated.

It is also disputed that, just as a good tree does not need to be forced to bear good fruit but does so naturally, so the justified should not be urged with the doctrine of the necessity to do good because they do it on their own, willingly and with utmost desire. But when the simple truth is sought, the explanation is straightforward. For in the regenerate man there is both the new man and the old man. About the new man, Paul says in Romans 7:22, "For I delight in the Law of God," and in Romans 6:17, "You have obeyed from the heart." About the old man, he says, "Putting to death, crucifying the old man." Also, "I discipline my body and bring it into subjection." And, "Taking every thought captive to obey Christ." This certainly means more than expressing under compulsion, especially concerning the old man. In regard to the new man, Paul says to Philemon in verse 14, "Your goodness should not be by compulsion but of your own free will." And in 1 Peter 5:2, "Not under compulsion, but willingly." 2 Corinthians 9:7 says, "Not reluctantly or under compulsion." These can certainly be explained distinctly so that the matters themselves can be understood without ambiguity.

This too is truly paradoxical. Indeed, good works are not necessary for salvation, but only renewal is necessary for salvation.

Finally, it must also be said about that proposition, "Good works are harmful to salvation,"* when it is posited plainly and bluntly like this, just as it is not simply false, but only in a certain respect, so it is not simply true, but only in a certain respect. However, in the Church, one should not indulge in such truncated and ambiguous paradoxes, which can hardly be explained with a lengthy, laborious, and careful interpretation, so as not to offend the ears of the pious and properly instructed. Rather, the norm and rule of speaking in the Church should be that true and necessary things are expressed simply and clearly, without ambiguity, so that even the unlearned can rightly understand them without commentaries.

When good works are accompanied by the notion of merit and confidence in righteousness before God; when good works are mixed into the article of Justification before God; when the question is what that thing is through which we reconcile with God and are accepted for eternal life; and, when the matter concerns the good works of the justified, considered in themselves and separate from faith, judged without mercy, such that imperfection is covered by faith, then the proposition [that is, "Good works are harmful to salvation."] is not only true but is the form of sound words. For it is expressed in this sentiment, and indeed it is almost repeated in those words, Philippians 3:7, "What things were gain to me, those I counted loss for Christ." Also verse 8, "I count all things to be loss for the

---

* Nicolaus von Amsdorf (1483–1565) originated this controversy. An early close confidant of Luther, Amsdorf was often involved in controversy. Luther consecrated as bishop of Naumberg in 1542, but lost his office in the aftermath of Luther's death and the Schmalkald War. In his latter years, Amsdorf was associated with the Gnesio-Lutherans of Magdeburg.

excellence of the knowledge." And, "for which I have suffered the loss of all things, and do count them but dung, that I may win Christ." Thus, Galatians 5:2, "If you are circumcised, Christ will profit you nothing; you are fallen from grace, you who are justified by the Law." Isaiah 66:3, "He who sacrifices a bull is as if he slays a man." Romans 9:31 and 11:7, "Israel, pursuing a law of righteousness, has not attained to the law of righteousness." Also, "What it sought, it did not obtain because not by faith, but as if by works." Galatians 3:10, "All who rely on observing the Law are under a curse." Isaiah 64:6, "All our righteousnesses are like filthy rags." And Augustine says, "Woe to the whole life of men, however praiseworthy, if judged without mercy." These are true and must necessarily be taught.

But it must be noted that Scripture does not present these propositions as truncated and bare, suggesting that the justified should avoid performing good works. Instead, Paul adds in Philippians 3:4, "I myself might have confidence in the flesh," which, [he continues in v. 8–9] "I consider a loss for the sake of Christ, and for the knowledge of Christ, ... to be found in Him, not having my own righteousness," [and] thus, I regard all things as loss." In Romans 9:32, "Because not from faith but as if from works." Hence, in pursuing the law of righteousness, they stumbled. As these are clearly presented, they are also correctly understood.

In the same way, there will be nothing inappropriate, and it will not offend any pious person, if the proposition is framed thus: "Good works, if done with the aim to earn salvation; if an opinion of merit, confidence, righteousness is added; if they are included in the article of Justification; if they carry the conviction that by their perfection they please God, and can be presented before the judgment of God, then they are harmful to salvation."

However, when the discussion concerns the reasons why the justified should perform good works; how they are to be exhorted to strive for good conduct; also, what place God holds for the good works of the justified, which are performed in true humility, acknowledging imperfection, and true faith seeking to have sins cleansed through Christ: then certainly it is not correct to say: Good works are harmful to salvation.

But they say, "We do not mean this." I respond, "Why, then, do they not rightly present what they feel—clearly, lucidly, and explicitly—so that it can be understood without ambiguity?" Certainly, this truncated and ambiguous proposition does not exist in the form of doctrine of our churches. And we have LUTHER's judgment on such propositions, for in Vol. 2, fol. 306, he disapproves of the Anabaptists' proposition: "We give all our good works for a penny."* And yet this proposition could be defended by a suitable interpretation. Why, then, does LUTHER reject it? The reason is clear, which also applies to the proposition currently under discussion. Thus, Urb. Rhegius on fol. 3 and 4 in the most useful booklet on forms of speaking carefully and without scandal, criticizes preachers who play with such truncated propositions: "There is nothing to our good works. They do not count. They stink before God. He does not want them."** And in the refutation, which he opposed to the Münsterites***, he teaches carefully how to clarify these propositions: "Faith alone makes blessed without good works. Also, faith can bear no good works with it".**** Such

---
* *"Wir geben alle unsere gute wercke umb einen groschen"*
** *"Es ist nichts mit unsern guten wercken: Sie gelten nicht: sie stincken für Gott: er wil ihr nicht"*
*** Chemnitz refers to the Anabaptists' 'kingdom' of Münster (1534–1535), a theocracy characterized by violence, polygamy, and primitive communism, which was ruled by a series of unhinged Anabaptists and which was finally brought to a conclusion by military siege and occupation. Münster became a Lutheran byword for Anabaptist governance.
**** *Der glaube machet selig ohne gute wercke/ Item / De Glaube kan keine gute wercke bey sich vertragen*

carefulness in speaking is necessary in the Church, for by the ambiguity of truncated propositions, the minds of teachers are distracted, learners are disturbed, the weak are offended, and the flesh is given pretext for recklessness. And what, pray tell, do such fervently disputed propositions accomplish, when in three words they could be so declared that the true meaning could be understood without ambiguity by anyone?

X.
On Adiaphora.*

In the dispute about this topic, the fallacy of multiple propositions introduces confusion. Therefore, the controversy should be stated distinctly regarding these issues.

Furthermore, it is beyond all controversy that in the Church, "adiaphora" are considered to be those rites which God in His Word neither commanded nor prohibited but left to the discretion of His Church under the general principle that they serve for decorum, order, discipline, edification, or acts of charity.

From this definition, it follows clearly:

1. Traditions that inherently conflict with God's Word and commandments, or that cannot be practiced without sin, are not to be counted among adiaphora because they are inherently impious and condemned.

2. Even when traditions deal with matters that are by nature indifferent, if they are accompanied by notions of worship, merit, necessity, or some impious superstition or demonic doctrine, they are not adiaphora.

3. Ridiculous and theatrical gestures, or idle and useless ceremonies, which serve neither discipline, decorum, nor order, but expose religion to ridicule and make people profane, are not considered under the term of "indifferent things," as we speak in the Church about adiaphora.

4. Ceremonies that are seedbeds of superstition, or cannot be used without superstition, or at least carry the appearance of

---

* See Formula of Concord Epitome and Solid Declaration, Article X, "Concerning Ecclesiastical Practices that are Called Adiaphora or Indifferent Things."

superstition, which they bring with their very use, do not pertain to the topic of adiaphora.

5. Nor should those rites be rightly called adiaphora, the observance of which strengthens the enemies of true doctrine and offends or weakens the less steadfast. Ceremonies should be aids, stimuli, and supports for true piety, edification, discipline, order, and decorum.

With these foundations laid, let us distinguish the questions so that we can properly establish the state of the controversy.

Therefore, the state of the controversies about this topic is *not* concerning this point: Whether all ecclesiastical ceremonies, which by their nature are not adiaphora and which serve order, are to be barbarously despised or universally abolished. Nor is the dispute about this proposition: When a pious consensus is retained in doctrinal purity, whether, in matters of faith and Christian truth, there can be diversity in those rites which by their nature are adiaphora, outside the case of scandal, according to each church's need for edification. We retain and approve the most beautiful opinion on this question, which exists in book 5, chapter 25, of *Ecclesiastical History*.* And we consider that churches should not be condemned because of such a difference in traditions. Moreover, it is undisputed that, for those who are weak and not yet confirmed in doctrine, who do not blaspheme or persecute it but are teachable and curable, something may be rightly be conceded in adiaphora out of charity (Rom. 14:15, 1 Cor. 8:9).

Moreover, regarding the rituals which are adiaphoristic by their nature, which were also customary under the papacy, as regards what can justly be conceded out of charity and brotherhood if the doctrine of faith is preserved, there exists Luther's opinion in his commentary on Galatians, folio 199. Also, in the fourth Ger-

---

* The reference is to the "Magdeburg Centuries" of Matthias Flacius Illyricus.

man volume, folios 382 and following: "For our part, to demonstrate that they do not seek unnecessary disputes through some kind of petulance, nor to dissent about adiaphoristic rites out of a desire to disagree or merely from a love of innovation, have often testified in many assemblies that if the purity of the Gospel is left to us, and consciences are not burdened with snares of necessity, or with superstitious and impious opinions, they will not fight over rituals that are adiaphora by nature. For Paul also, to show that he was not fighting against the Mosaic rites as things inherently impious, if the truth of the Gospel is preserved and consciences are not burdened with snares of necessity or other impious opinions, shaved his head, undertook a vow, and purified himself (Acts 18:18 and 21:26). Therefore, the controversies of recent years concerning adiaphora did not arise from these questions."

But the status of the controversy is this: It is certain that deliberations about adiaphora arose from the proposed formula of the Augsburg Interim [*Interreligionis Augustanae*], and because that book, among other things, demanded the restoration and conformity of all rites that are customary under the papacy. It is also certain by what counsel, and to what end, this book was proposed under the insidious appearance of moderation. These are indeed the words in the preface, in the report of the Emperor: "From the highly harmful contentious division of religion has resulted, and is also still to be expected, all detrimental mistrust, war, opposition, distress, burden, disadvantage, impoverishment, damage, and ruin of the German nation. Therefore, the highest and unavoidable necessity demands not to leave this matter stuck or hanging in the current state and confusion, but for your Christian reconciliation and moderation, and for better and more understanding to be directed." And lest there be doubt whether these things are to be understood concerning the Papists, or rather those who profess the doctrine of the Augsburg Confession, it immediately adds, "The estates that have up to now maintained the ordinances of the common Christian Church shall also continue to maintain them hereafter, and not deviate from them, nor undertake changes." This is a severe condemnation of our doctrine and a loud proclamation that through the Interim, the eradication of the Gospel doctrine is sought, and the restoration of the kingdom of the Antichrist.

Therefore, adiaphora were proposed and demanded in the Interim book, not due to the right of charity, nor the duty of fraternity, nor for the sake of order, decorum, or discipline—as if to be supports or safeguards for true piety and sound doctrine—but so that by their restoration we might profess that we had grievously sinned by their omission and abolition. Also, because the sound doctrine, which is summed up in the Augsburg Confession, seemed to have taken deeper roots in the minds of the pious than could be suddenly uprooted in one strike, a conformism in adiaphoric rites was insidiously contrived under the guise of moderation, so as thus to prepare the way by which, with the spirits of the faithful first weakened, a fuller adherence would follow to those changes in doctrine proposed in the Interim book. And thus, eventually, through the soon-to-follow Council of Trent, to whose decrees our people were to bind themselves to approve and observe before knowing the matter, the doctrine of the Augsburg Confession would be utterly extinguished and eradicated, and the kingdom of the Antichrist with all its abominations would be completely restored: "For this is called directing towards moderation and a better understanding," in the proclamation of the Emperor.

The question now is: In such a case, could anything in adiaphora have been conceded to the adversaries with faith preserved and a good conscience, when those adversaries explicitly professed that they were seeking, then and by that very demand, the abolition of true doctrine and the restoration of all the abominations of the

Papal kingdom? For with what mind and with what opinion the Interim demanded restoration and conformity in adiaphora, we will show with its own words. The bishops explicitly declared, "We understand it to be intended in such a way that it should conform with the formula" prescribed by the Emperor. Moreover, by this concession and change, the party that thinks correctly has become weakened, and the errant and adversaries strengthened, so much so that it was manifestly and notably set forth several times in the Acts of the Synod. This is the state of the controversy, namely, whether in such a case, even in rites that are in themselves indifferent, something ought to have been conceded to the adversaries by way of restoration and conformity, especially in the extreme turmoil of all affairs and the nearly desperate calamity of the common homeland.

Such sudden dismay had seized nearly all minds that it is not surprising that even great men* suffered something human, acting more languidly than the standard of the Word of God requires and the case of the confession [*casus confessionis*] demands in indifferent matters, especially in those where it was judged that a concession could be made without harm to the faith. For even Peter, such a great Apostle, surrounded by lesser terror and danger, was led into dissimulation by the concession of indifferent matters in a similar case, as we will soon discuss. But having been admonished, he did not defend what he had committed against the apostolic teaching on adiaphora, merely with a weakening of the correct opinion and a strengthening of the errant. Nor is anything else now sought but that the true doctrine of indifferent matters, which was established from the Word of God in the [Augsburg] Confession, Apology, in *Common Places***, and in other writings be-

---

* e.g., Philip Melanchthon and Johannes Bugenhagen.
** Chemnitz emphasizes that works written by Melanchthon—the Augsburg Confession, Apology, and the *Loci Communes* (*Common Places*)—provide the model for Christian doctrine and practice regarding this matter. Chemnitz

fore these controversies, be preserved uncorrupted, and that deliberations and actions which conflict with that doctrine not be defended. And so far, the disputes have been about this act, which was reproached because it does not conform to the form of the doctrine of indifferent matters.

Now indeed, the action is defended in such a way that the doctrine of adiaphora is undeniably distorted. For even during the time of persecution, this courtly wisdom prevailed, such that in a time of chaos, nothing but danger, war, and other calamities would follow a steadfast and honest confession of the truth. Therefore, they argued that through pretense, especially in matters of indifference, the purity of the doctrine could be safeguarded and restored with less risk and greater certainty should fortunes change. And now* they boldly claim that in matters of indifference, it does not matter how, in what situation, or with what intentions and beliefs the observance of adiaphora is perceived and understood by others, whether they are friends or foes, as long as the matters themselves are by nature indifferent, and the intentions of those adopting or enforcing the adiaphora are not evil or impious. This is a blatant corruption of the doctrine of adiaphora, which must be countered.

For it must not be thought that it does not matter whatever is done, established, and taught about adiaphora, in any case, provided that the necessary articles of the doctrine are retained else-

---

argues that Melanchthon—like Peter—failed in a particular circumstance to uphold that which he taught. Chemnitz's treatment of the issue demonstrates that he was free of the *rabies theologica* that afflicted Flacius and other so-called Gnesio-Lutherans.

* Chemnitz now changes focus to those who are presently continuing to teach a false understanding of adiaphora. (Years before his death in 1560, Melanchthon wrote to Flacius: "I have sinned in this matter and ask forgiveness of God." Like St. Peter, Melanchthon repented of his error. However, Flacius used Melanchthon's confession to continue to attack him—a matter which offended Chemnitz and other faithful theologians.)

where. For Paul says about adiaphora in Romans 14:6, "He who observes the day, observes it in honor of the Lord. He who eats, eats in honor of the Lord, since he gives thanks to God, while he who abstains, abstains in honor of the Lord and gives thanks to God." Also in verse 13, "Let us not therefore judge one another anymore." And in 1 Corinthians 7:19, "Circumcision is nothing and uncircumcision is nothing." Paul also says about things that are by nature indifferent in Galatians 4:11, "I am afraid I may have labored over you in vain." Galatians 5:2, "Behold I, Paul, say to you that if you accept circumcision, Christ will be of no advantage to you." In Galatians 2:5—speaking about a matter which is by nature indifferent (as he proved in Romans 14:6)—Paul says, "To them we did not yield submission even for a moment, that the truth of the Gospel might continue with you." Therefore, such cases can exist in adiaphora that, by the acceptance and use of things that are by nature indifferent, the truth of the Gospel is lost, and the treasure of Christ's benefits is taken from us and made void. Therefore, one must not play with adiaphora lightly, in any case. For adiaphora can become so necessary that the truth of the Gospel and the fruit of Christ's benefits cannot be retained unless one fights seriously against adiaphora and shows examples of Christian liberty.

However, in the Word of God we have a certain and explicit standard for judging this case. For in Galatians 2:11 and following, Peter, who had shown an example of Christian liberty at Antioch among the Gentiles by eating foods forbidden by Moses, faced certain false brothers who had slipped in to spy out our Christian liberty and were pressing for Mosaic observances, not out of a law of love and in the spirit of brotherhood, but because they judged that by omitting these observances, consciences would be sinning; and under this guise, they gradually instilled in minds the opinion that we are justified not by faith alone but also by observance of the Law being necessary for salvation, as stated in Acts 15,:1. When they came to Antioch, Peter began to withdraw himself from the Gentiles, fearing those who were of the circumcision. However, it is certain beyond all controversy that Peter did not do this out of an impious belief in necessity, worship, merit, or righteousness; nor was it his intention by this act to prove, admit, or accept the adversaries' corruptions regarding the article of Justification, or to betray the truth of the Gospel. For Paul calls it hypocrisy, to show that Peter felt differently than how that external appearance was received and understood by both the adversaries and the insiders of the faith. Then Paul, with great severity, publicly before everyone, reproached Peter because of that concession, although it was concerning a matter that by its nature is adiaphora and was done by Peter not out of an impious belief. Yet he says Peter was reprehensible because he did it on account of those who pressed such observances with an impious belief and insidious pretense. And although Peter did not harbor ill thoughts within himself, yet because by the appearance of concession the adversaries were confirmed in their errors, and the weak were scandalized, and Barnabas and others were led into hypocrisy, therefore, Paul withstood Peter to his face, and the reason is that by that act Peter did not walk straightforwardly according to the truth of the Gospel. Also, "that the truth of the Gospel might continue with you." [Gal. 2:5]

Therefore, it is certain and evident that in matters of adiaphora, not only these two things must be considered: 1. What things by their nature are adiaphora [ἀδιάφοροι]. 2. What opinion and conscience the person who receives the adiaphora uses them. Thus, Peter would not have sinned in Galatians 2:13. But, especially during times of persecution, and when false brothers insinuate themselves, and when it is sought and acted upon to either by force, deceit, or cunning, obscure, adulterate, or extinguish the purity of doctrine, then it must be considered: 1. Who are those demanding concessions in adiaphora, and with what opinion adiaphora are proposed, pressed, or mandated. 2. If enemies or adversaries are indeed confirmed in their position by concessions in adiaphora. 3. If the weak and not yet sufficiently confirmed are disturbed or scandalized by that appearance, so that they might begin to doubt the entire body of doctrine or lean towards defection.

These [points] are very clear from the case of Peter, which Paul says in Galatians 2:11was reprehensible. And from this example of Peter, the judgment of this controversy should be taken, not from a strange allegory of John 21:18, as the sophists do.

And it must be carefully observed what Paul says, that the truth of the Gospel might remain with you. Also, he does not "walk straight according to the truth of the Gospel." [Gal. 2:14] For some do not hesitate to assert that by that concession in adiaphora during the INTERIM period, the purity of the Evangelical doctrine was preserved, and that in such a case, concessions can be made to retain the truth of the Gospel—although Paul expressly affirms the contrary about such a case.

This also pertains to the doctrine of adiaphora: When either openly or insidiously the true doctrine is corrupted, then even with rituals which by themselves and by their nature are adiaphora, a state of confession [*casus confessionis*] is connected. Also, when something is commanded out of an impious belief, Christian piety requires not a simulation in external appearance, while internally feeling rightly, but an honest confession. For what would confession be, if it were permissible to simulate one thing openly in external appearance, and secretly feel another? And concerning the case of confession in adiaphora, there are examples from Daniel 3:16 and 6:10, and of Eleazar in 2 Maccabees 6:21. Also the example of Jovinian, when he was sprinkled with lustral water. Also Marcellinus, who had protested that he did not throw incense into the fire with the belief in sacrificing; yet he later rightly condemned his own action. And these examples of demonstrating the use of freedom in such cases exist in *Common Places*.* LUTHER also in a similar case accurately and extensively explained this doctrine in Volume 4, German edition, folio 378.

However, it is well known that in the case of confession during the Interim period of persecution, the sin was not only in matters of adiaphora, but also in the doctrine itself. For the courtly document presented in Leipzig** had so recast the entire formula of doctrine in its principal articles to suit the palate of the Papists that the pontifical bishops, who in public confession professed to understand that formula in such a way as to show and establish consensus with the writing of the Augsburg Interim, did not abhor it. For the form of sound words, which had previously been accepted and used in the Augsburg Confession and other writings of ours to cover the abomination of the Papacy and to illuminate the proper doctrine of the Gospel, was studiously altered and expunged, and the language and speech of the Papal Church were simulated. Certain twistings of speech were intermixed with brevity and ambiguity to give the Papists the appearance that our people would gradually return to the bosom of the Roman pontiff, and among our own people, not yet sufficiently safeguarded and confirmed, they could gradually lead away from the purity of the word to the idolatry of the Papacy.

If they object, claiming they felt otherwise, more correctly and better, the true, solid, and straightforward response is: It is not a true confession to feel one way and speak another, and especially towards those [errors] where a confession is required with words,

* Chemnitz is noting that regardless of the criticisms of Melanchthon's actions during the Interim, his teaching in his *Loci Communes*/*Common Places* on this subject is quite sound.
** For an English translation of the Leipzig document, see H.E. Jacobs, *Book of Concord*, 2 vols., vol. 2 (Decatur, Illinois: Johann Gerhard Institute, 1996), p. 290–302.

gestures, rites, and any external appearance. Likewise, to openly or publicly cease the reproach and refutation of errors, and meanwhile, in private, secretive meetings, where confession is not so required, to murmur and debate about retaining the true doctrine and refuting the contrary. For Scripture describes confession thus: "With the heart one believes and is justified, and with the mouth one confesses and is saved." Also, "I believed, therefore I have spoken." And what it is to sin in the matter of confession is shown by that grim sentence in Matthew 10:33.

These foundations are true, solid, and clear, and whatever deliberations or actions fight against these scriptural foundations should not be defended with a harmful example for posterity. Much less should it be allowed that, for the sake of defending things which were acted upon less correctly, the true and clear sentence of Scripture be evaded, obscured, and corrupted, as is now the case.

And we must diligently beware, since our churches have been rescued from those papal snares, not to think that God, because of that vacillation, either approved it or did not care, [since] He has bestowed upon us this great benefit. But let us recognize our weaknesses and our shortcomings, ask for forgiveness, and give thanks to God, who has not dealt with us according to our iniquities, but with immense mercy for the glory of His name, and through the intercession of our Lord Jesus Christ, corrected our shortcomings, and thwarted and broke the efforts of our adversaries. And let us pray that by His Holy Spirit He may govern all who teach and learn in the future, that in peaceful times we may calmly teach and learn what is true and useful; and that in the oncoming storms of persecution, with His help, we may be able to glorify God the Father of our Lord Jesus Christ by a steadfast confession of the truth, and through His grace preserve the purity of doctrine and propagate it to posterity. Thus will be established a concord pleasing to God, useful to the Church, and salutary to posterity.

The foundations of the controversy concerning the Lord's Supper are noted elsewhere, namely in my booklet, which is titled *Repetition of the Sound Doctrine of the Lord's Supper*.* In Brunswick, in the Year of Christ 1561, 3 days before the Calends of April.

---

* English translation published as *A Repetition of the Sound Doctrine: Concerning the True Presence of the Body and Blood of the Lord in the Supper*, trans. by Paul A. Rydecki, (Malone, Texas: Repristination Press, 2021).

www.ingramcontent.com/pod-product-compliance
Lightning Source LLC
Chambersburg PA
CBHW062115080426
42734CB00012B/2870